Henry James

Interviews and Recollections

HENRY JAMES

Interviews and Recollections

Edited by

Norman Page

St. Martin's Press   **New York**

ISBN 0-312-36899-2

Library of Congress Cataloging in Publication Data

Main entry under title:

Henry James.

Includes index.
1. James Henry, 1843-1916 – Biography.   2. James,
Henry, 1843-1916 – Friends and associates.
3. Authors, American – 19th century – Biography.
I. James, Henry, 1843-1916.   II. Page, Norman.
PS2123.H45 1984   813′.4 [B]   83-16111
ISBN 0-312-36899-2

Contents

Acknowledgements

The editor and publishers wish to thank the following who have kindly given permission for the use of copyright material:

George Allen & Unwin (Publishers) Ltd, for the extract from *Looking Down the Years* by Raymond Blathwayt.

Constable & Co. Ltd, for the extract from *Max* by David Cecil.

Dodd, Mead & Co. Inc., for the extract from *The Diary of Alice James*, edited by Leon Edel.

Faber & Faber Ltd, for the extract from *Experiment in Autobiography: Discoveries and Conclusions of a Very Ordinary Brain*, by H. G. Wells.

Hamish Hamilton Ltd, for the extracts from *Time Was* by W. Graham Robertson, and *A Number of People* by Edward Marsh.

David Higham Associates Ltd, on behalf of the Literary Estate of Ford Madox Ford, for the extract from *Thus to Revisit: Some Reminiscences*.

The Hogarth Press Ltd, on behalf of the Literary Estate of Theodora Bosanquet, for the extract from *Henry James at Work*, and the Literary Estate of Virginia Woolf, for the extract from *The Flight of the Mind: The Letters of Virginia Woolf*, vol. 1: *1888–1912*, edited by Nigel Nicolson.

Mrs Isobel Garland Lord and Mrs Constance Garland Doyle, for the extract from *Roadside Meetings* by the late Hamlin Garland.

The MacNaughton Lowe Representation, 'or the extract from 'Henry James: a Reminiscence' by Hugh Walpole.

The *Mark Twain Quarterly*, for the extract from the article 'Henry James at Dinner' by Elizabeth Jordan (1943).

John Murray (Publishers) Ltd, for the extract from *John Bailey, 1864–1931: Letters and Diaries*.

The Society of Authors, as the Literary Representative of the Estate of Sir Compton Mackenzie, for the extract from 'Henry James' in *Life and Letters Today*.

A. P. Watt Ltd, on behalf of the Executors of the Estate of E. F. Benson, for the extracts from *As We Were* and *Final Edition*, and on behalf of Miss D. E. Collins, for the extract from *Autobiography* by G. K. Chesterton.

Every effort has been made to trace all the copyright-holders but if any have been inadvertently overlooked, the publishers will be pleased to make the necessary arrangement at the first opportunity.

Introduction

Henry James was a man of wide and sometimes deep friendships: Hugh Walpole, indeed, speaks of 'his passion for his friends'.[1] Fortunately for us, many of those friends, as well as many more casual acquaintances, found his doings, and especially his sayings, so interesting that they recorded them in their letters and diaries, and so memorable that they recalled them, sometimes long after the event, in their autobiographies and reminiscences. James had no Boswell, but the collective testimony of those who knew him is very extensive; attempts to record his conversation are particularly numerous, and probably no other major novelist is known to us so fully in his habit as he talked. As with Dr Johnson, however, the bulk of this material relates to his later years; the record of James's first half-century is relatively sparse, though some vivid glimpses have been preserved – for example, the enchanted and enchanting moment with which this selection opens, set down later by his sister Alice (herself a remarkable member of a remarkable family).

For that reason it has seemed best not to attempt to present these extracts chronologically but to arrange them roughly according to topic. During his early years in England, James lived mainly in London, conscientiously moving in society, but he also paid frequent and sometimes prolonged visits to the Continent. He was bearded at this time, and Max Beerbohm, who met him in 1895, 'thought he looked "like a Russian Grand Duke of the better type" and was struck by his curious "veiled" expression'.[2] Max, who often encountered James when dining out, set down further impressions in his notebook:

> Delightful company – you had to wait – worth it – very literary – enormous vocabulary – great manner, as in books – never smiles – rather appalled by life – cloistral ... priest – fine eyes – magnificent head – ... strong voice – holding table.[3]

The present volume includes recollections of James's social life in London and elsewhere – a life mainly urban, as is illustrated by an entry in William Allingham's diary dated 19 August 1888, referring to an al fresco tea-party at which James was present:

> The Anglo–American novelist had just arrived from London, and was going back by a late train.
>
> He described himself as an 'unmitigated Cockney', was surprised at the colour of the heather, and hearing ling spoken of, asked to look at it.[4]

This was the James who in a review of Hardy's *Far from the Madding Crowd* had spoken patronisingly of 'a certain aroma of the meadows and lanes – a natural relish for harvesting and sheep-washings'.

After settling at Lamb House, Rye, in 1898, James spent less time in London: but his hospitality was generous, and there was no shortage of visitors to enjoy his company and in due course to recall it. Around the turn of the century he shaved off his beard; in his later years he seems also to have put on a good deal of weight and came to resemble a well-fed abbé (a frequent comparison). The artist William Rothenstein described him during the Rye years:

> Henry James, massive in face and figure, slow and impressive in speech, had now become one of the great pundits, to whom ladies sat listening in adoration; pilgrimages were made to his house at Rye; his dicta, elaborate, wise and tortuous, were repeated in clubs and drawing rooms.[5]

Of James in middle age and old age, many social moments have been recorded: of his being told a ghost story by the Archbishop of Canterbury, meeting Thomas Hardy at the Athenaeum, watching (or not watching) a cricket match, running into Virginia Woolf in Rye High Street, and being punted on the Cam by Rupert Brooke. There are also vignettes of an informality that the Master might have deplored: awaiting a visit from his chiropodist, sitting in a red undershirt during a heatwave, having his hair cut in the company of J. M. Barrie, eating haggis while wearing a paper hat found in a Christmas cracker, and ponderously ordering marmalade at the urging of his patient but persistent housekeeper.[6]

All this, however, was on or near the periphery of a life continuously and indefatigably devoted to the pursuit of art; and it is to his comments on his work and on the work of other writers that some of the most suggestive passages of recollection refer. We are, again, fortunate that for a number of years his secretary was Theodora Bosanquet: the soul of stenographic discretion, she knew her place but was also a lively and perceptive young woman whose *Henry James at Work* is based on a sustained sharing of a great writer's workshop that is a very rare experience.

It is, though, for the records of his conversation that we are most likely to quarry the voluminous recollections of James; and the search is richly rewarded. James's talk was inexhaustibly witty and, although a recognisable and readily-parodied Jamesian manner developed, infinitely surprising. To be sure, it was less conversation than monologue: as Alfred Sutro said, James 'belonged to the buttonholing school, he would suddenly stand still and talk at you and you had to keep your eyes fixed on his and stand still with him'.[7] Another listener recalled his dominating the conversational as well as the physical scene:

[At the Kensington home of Sidney Lee,] all the guests were intellectuals, but I remember none but Henry James, who filled the eye as well as the ear. He talked all the time, talked coherently, brilliantly, illuminatingly. Nobody wanted to listen to anyone else, and if a pause threatened he was gently prodded. Alas, that I should have forgotten what he talked about![8]

That last sentence has a rare honesty. All too often writers of reminiscences implicitly lay claim to the gift of total recall. We can believe without too much difficulty that James's more succinct witticisms may have been transmitted accurately – for instance, his Wildean description of two fellow-novelists as 'Meredith the Obscure and the Amazing Hardy'[9] – though even here there is scope for error. Different informants inspire in the reader very different degrees of confidence: for example, Elizabeth Jordan's account of James's table-talk (p. 74) has the ring of authenticity, but it is difficult to believe that he announced baldly to Hamlin Garland that he was 'a lonely man' (p. 91). Occasionally a saying has been committed to paper before the memory has had time to fade:

I shall never forget Henry James the novelist explaining to Henry Morley how he strayed off the road when visiting his brother William in Chocorua: 'I had been *lost* had not a peasant emerged from the wood with a bundle of faggots upon his shoulder, and directed me to the Post.' (I am no Boswell, but *I did write that sentence down!*)[10]

Not all, however, were so prompt at taking up the pen or so scrupulous in defining the bounds of their accuracy. Some admit to being able to give no more than a faint impression of James's conversational manner, and this at least is honest. Joseph Pennell, the illustrator, offers a delightful sample without making pretence of a feat of memory that would clearly be implausible. Pennell suggested to James 'points of view from which to see New York', including the top of the Singer Building, 'then the highest in the world'; but James retorted that skyscrapers 'were not for him':

> 'But for you – they are yours to draw, – but – ah – oh – just to think of it – difficult, yes, no, impossible, forty skyscrapers – each forty stories – each story forty windows – each window forty people – each person forty tales – My God – maddening – what could I, or am I – yes – certainly, no, of course – do with such a thing?' I cannot get any nearer to it, and only those who knew him will understand.[11]

The fallibility of memory and the hubris of memoirists can be demonstrated from a single oft-recounted incident. Writing in 1925, Pennell recalled James's description of two lady visitors as 'sad wantons, one of whom was not without a pale cadaverous grace'. The following year C. Lewis Hind reported the remark in a slightly different form ('One of the wantons had a certain languorous grace'), and a few years later E. F. Benson published yet another version ('there were some faint traces of bygone beauty on the face of one of the two poor wantons'). Since the incident in question took place in 1899, all of these were reporting a remark a generation old; since none of them (it seems) was present on the occasion, all were reporting it at second or more distant hand. In 1931, a letter by Sir Edmund Gosse 'written within a few days, if not a few hours, of the utterance of the *mot*' was published. Gosse's version is: 'One of the poor wantons had a certain cadaverous grace.' (Later still, a more dramatic version was offered by the notoriously unreliable Ford Madox Ford, who describes James, 'with a face working with fury', exclaiming, 'A couple of jaded ... WANTONS!') Comparison of these five versions speaks for itself and carries its own warning.[12]

The highly idiosyncratic conversational style seems to have established itself relatively early, for in the summer of 1886 we find Hardy noting in his diary a meeting of the Rabelais Club at which a fellow-diner was James, 'who has a ponderously warm manner of saying nothing in infinite sentences'.[13] Meredith was also present. The amplitude of James's slow delivery, his hesitations and repetitions, his groping for the unpredictable but satisfyingly apt word, his rejection of inferior locutions, were features of a style that one would call inimitable if it had not been so frequently imitated. To the list might be added his disinclination or inability to express a simple idea briefly or directly, were it not that on occasion he could be superbly succinct (see, for example, his comment on George Eliot's widower: p. 33 below).

James had a considerable appetite for gossip that was partly a manifestation of genuine interest in the lives of his friends. In February 1885, Gosse wrote to William Dean Howells:

> Last week I dined with Henry James at the Reform Club, to satisfy his craving for gossip, which proved insatiable ... he was eager to know every little tiny thing that had befallen us, and what 'poor' everybody said and was doing, and in fact was a most agreeable recipient of all that I was primed with.[14]

James's appetite for 'every little tiny thing' was also, however, part of his daily business as a novelist. At the same time, he was not innocent of malice, or at least mischief – of that 'deep-seated felinity' that he attributed to Edmund Gosse (see p. 122). E. V. Lucas recalled:

> I met him only once, late in his life, at Lady Colvin's. He led me aside and was very malicious. In the choicest of words, so carefully chosen that one was in an agony of fear he should fail to find them, changing and refining all the time and postponing the end of the sentence to the last possible moment, he said something detrimental about most of the company. But that was only his way, I think. He must have been very kind underneath or he wouldn't have been so much liked and even loved.[15]

Near the end of James's life, the outbreak of war had a profound emotional impact upon him. H. H. Asquith recalled that 'he never concealed for a moment his ardent sympathy with the Allies and their cause'.[16] The national crisis seemed to bring into the open his deep attachment to his adopted country (Arnold Bennett noted that 'Henry James is strongly pro-English, and comes to weeping-point sometimes'[17]), and his naturalisation was a logical but also a consciously symbolic act.

His long drawn-out dying and the last-minute bestowal of the Order of Merit constitute a moving story. Virginia Woolf recorded his death in a letter:

Henry James is dead. His last words, according to Sydney [Water-low], were to his secretary, whom he sent for. 'I wish to dictate a few faint and faded words – ' after which he was silent and never spoke again.[18]

Like his reported response to the news that the King had bestowed upon him the OM, this need not necessarily be taken at face value: the master of the art of fiction was to the very end himself the object of a largely unconscious fictionalising process. Historical or not, however, the story is finely in character and epitomises that sense of style that belonged to James's life as well as to his art and infused even his least momentous pronouncements. It is not everyone who could contrive to stamp his unmistakable individuality upon a nine-word telegram:

Henry James and telegraphy do not naturally suggest themselves as associates, but here is a telegram to Abbey from the great master of leisurely and sufficient verbosity:
'Will alight precipitately at 5.38 from the deliberate 1.50.'[19]

The purpose of the present volume is to bring together many aspects of that individuality, transmitted by a large number of those who knew him.

Any work on the life of Henry James must owe a great debt to the five volumes of Leon Edel's biography (London: Hart-Davis, 1953–72). References are abbreviated as follows:

Untried Years – Henry James, the Untried Years: 1843–1870 (1953).
Conquest of London – Henry James, the Conquest of London: 1870–1881 (1962).
Middle Years – Henry James, the Middle Years: 1882–1895 (1962).
Treacherous Years – Henry James, the Treacherous Years: 1895–1901 (1969).
Master – Henry James, the Master: 1901–1916 (1972).

For bibliographical information, I am indebted to Leon Edel and Dan H. Laurence, *A Bibliography of Henry James* (London: Hart-Davis, 1961). The bibliography in Simon Nowell-Smith's *The Legend of the Master* (London: Constable, 1947) has also been useful. Mr Nowell-Smith's collection has long been out of print and is in any case mainly confined to short extracts; the task he did so well has therefore seemed worth undertaking again with somewhat different principles in mind as well as with the advantage of access to material that has become available during the past thirty years.

American spellings have been anglicised and obvious errors in the original texts have been silently corrected.

NOTES

1. See p. 22.
2. David Cecil, *Max* (London: Constable, 1964) p. 154.
3. Ibid., p. 211.
4. William Allingham, *Diary*, ed. H. Allingham and D. Radford (London: Macmillan, 1907) p. 378.
5. William Rothenstein, *Men and Memories, 1872–1922* (London: Faber, 1931–2) II, p. 173.
6. Joseph Pennell recounts visiting James at his London flat during a heat-wave and finding him 'standing at a high writing desk in a dark room, in a red undershirt'; he also describes James at a Christmas dinner given by Sir Frederick Macmillan in 1912 (*The Adventures of an Illustrator* (London: Fisher Unwin, 1925) pp. 259, 264). The other episodes are included in this selection.
7. Alfred Sutro, *Celebrities and Simple Souls* (London: Duckworth, 1933) p. 181.
8. Gertrude Atherton, *Adventures of a Novelist* (London: Cape, 1932) p. 363.
9. Michael Field, *Works and Days* (London: Murray, 1922) p. 201.
10. Bliss Perry, *And Gladly Teach* (Boston, Mass.: Houghton Mifflin, 1935) p. 290.
11. Joseph Pennell, *Adventures of an Illustrator*, p. 264.
12. In his excellent introduction to *The Legend of the Master*, Simon Nowell-Smith quotes the examples from Pennell, Benson and Gosse (pp. xxii, xxvi, xxvii). Hind's version appears on p. 114 below, and Ford's in *Mightier than the Sword* (London: Allen & Unwin, 1938) p. 29.
13. F. E. Hardy, *The Life of Thomas Hardy, 1840–1928* (London: Macmillan, 1962) p. 181. Hardy's first reference to a meeting with James is at the beginning of 1880, when they were both present (together with Matthew Arnold and Richard Jefferies) at a dinner given by a publisher (*Life*, p. 164). They met again quite frequently on social and formal occasions – for example, at a masked ball in 1896, 'when he and Henry James were the only two not in dominoes, and were recklessly flirted with by the women in consequence' (p. 276). For Hardy's disingenuous account of James's association with the Rabelais Club (founded by Sir Walter Besant with the curious object of promoting virility in literature), see p. 132 of the *Life*. Hardy's last reference to a meeting with James is in his account of the Westminster Abbey memorial service for Meredith held in May 1909 (p. 346). After the posthumous publication of James's letters, Hardy was much offended by his remarks in a letter to R. L. Stevenson concerning *Tess of the d'Urbervilles* (p. 246); Hardy refers to James and Stevenson as 'the Polonius and the Osric of novelists'. He also repeats the canard that in 1880 Mrs Procter, the famous literary hostess, then eighty years old, showed him a photograph of Henry James and declared that the latter had made her an offer of marriage.

14. Evan Charteris, *The Life and Letters of Sir Edmund Gosse* (London: Heinemann, 1931) p. 178.

15. E. V. Lucas, *Reading, Writing and Remembering* (London: Methuen, 1932) pp. 183–4.

16. Earl of Oxford & Asquith, *Memories & Reflections, 1852–1937* (London: Cassell, 1928) I, p. 283.

17. Arnold Bennett, *Journals*, ed. Newman Flower (London: Cassell, 1932–3) II, p. 108.

18. *The Question of Things Happening: The Letters of Virginia Woolf*, vol. II: *1912–1922*, ed. Nigel Nicolson (London: Hogarth Press, 1976) p. 84 (letter to Katherine Cox, dated 19 March 1916).

19. E. V. Lucas, *E. A. Abbey, Royal Academician: The Record of his Life and Work* (London: Methuen, 1921) I, p. 268.

A Henry James Chronology

(Only a selection of James's voluminous publications are noted; dates are of first volume publication, English or American.)

1843   (15 April) Henry James born in New York, second son of Henry James, theologian, and Mary Robertson James, and younger brother of William James (born 1842), who became a famous philosopher and psychologist.

1843–5   First visit to Europe.

1845–55   Lives in Albany (New York State) and New York.

1855–60   Lives mainly in Geneva, London, Paris, Boulogne and Bonn, with an extended visit to America in 1858–9. Returns to America in the autumn of 1860.

1861   (12 April) Civil War begins; (October) in helping to put out a fire, Henry James suffers a 'physical mishap' referred to much later as an 'obscure hurt' and identified by Leon Edel as a back injury.

1862–3   Attends Harvard Law School.

1864   The James family move to Boston. (February) Henry James publishes his first story, 'A Tragedy of Error' (uncollected); (October) publishes his first review. Meets William Dean Howells and Charles Eliot Norton.

1866   The James family move to Cambridge, Massachusetts.

1869–70   James visits England, France, Switzerland and Italy. (March 1870) Hears of the death of his cousin Minnie Temple.

1871   *Watch and Ward*, James's first novel, is serialised in the *Atlantic Monthly*.

1872–4   Lives in Europe again, spending the winters in Italy and the summers in Germany and Switzerland.

1875   Lives in New York. (November) Settles in Paris; meets Turgenev, Flaubert, Zola, Daudet, Maupassant. Publishes (January) *A Passionate Pilgrim* (stories); (April) *Transatlantic Sketches*; (November) *Roderick Hudson*.

1876	Settles in London but continues to pay frequent visits to the Continent.
1877	(May) *The American* published.
1878	(February) *French Poets and Novelists*; (May) *Watch and Ward* (volume edition), (September) *The Europeans*, and (November) *Daisy Miller* published.
1879	(October) *The Madonna of the Future* (stories) and (December) *Hawthorne* (biography in English Men of Letters series) published.
1880	(January) *A Bundle of Letters* and (December) *Washington Square* published.
1881	(October) Visits America. (November) *The Portrait of a Lady* published.
1882	(January) Death of James's mother; (May) he returns to London; (December) death of James's father; he revisits America.
1883	(August) Returns to London. (February) *The Siege of London* (stories) and (December) *Portraits of Places* published. Collective Edition of James's works (cheap edition in fourteen volumes) appears in November.
1884	(September) *A Little Tour in France* published; essay 'The Art of Fiction' appears in *Longman's Magazine*. Alice James (sister, born 1848) arrives in England.
1885	(February) *The Author of Beltraffio* (stories) and (May) *Stories Revived* published.
1886	James settles in his London flat at 34 De Vere Gardens, Kensington. (February) *The Bostonians* and (October) *The Princess Casamassima* published.
1887	(February–July) Spends several months in Venice.
1888	(October) Visits Switzerland. (May) *Partial Portraits*, (June) *The Reverberator* and (September) *The Aspern Papers* (stories) published.
1889	(April) *A London Life* (stories) published.
1890	(June) *The Tragic Muse* published.
1891	(3 January) *The American* (James's dramatisation of his novel) produced; it opens in London on 26 September.
1892	(6 March) Death of Alice James. (February) *The Lesson of the Master* published.
1893	(March) *The Real Thing* and (June) *The Private Life* (volumes of stories) published.
1894	(June, December) *Theatricals* published in two volumes (two plays in each volume, all unproduced).

1895	(5 January) *Guy Domville* produced. (May) *Terminations* (stories) published.
1896	(June) *Embarrassments* (stories) and (October) *The Other House* published.
1897	James leases (and later buys) Lamb House at Rye in Sussex, and thereafter spends most summers there. (February) *The Spoils of Poynton* and (September) *What Maisie Knew* published.
1898	(August) *In the Cage* published.
1899	(April) *The Awkward Age* published.
1900	(August) *The Soft Side* (stories) published.
1901	(February) *The Sacred Fount* published.
1902	(August) *The Wings of the Dove* published.
1903	(February) *The Better Sort* (stories) and (September) *The Ambassadors* published.
1904	James visits America for the first time since 1883. (November) *The Golden Bowl* published.
1905	In America, James visits California, Florida, Chicago, etc., and lectures in Philadelphia and elsewhere. (October) *English Hours* published.
1906–8	James revises his novels and stories and writes new critical prefaces for a collected edition (the New York Edition), published in twenty-four volumes (1907–9).
1907	(January) *The American Scene* published.
1909–10	(winter) James is seriously ill.
1909	(October) *Italian Hours* published.
1910–11	Last visit to America. William James dies on 26 August 1910. Henry James returns to England in August 1911.
1910	(October) *The Finer Grain* (stories) published.
1912	James receives the honorary degree of Doctor of Letters from the University of Oxford.
1913	(March) *A Small Boy and Others* published.
1914	(March) *Notes on a Son and Brother* and (October) *Notes on Novelists* published.
1915	(26 July) James becomes a naturalised British citizen. (2 and 3 December) He suffers two strokes and is confined to his bed.
1916	(1 January) Award of the Order of Merit announced. (28 February) Death of Henry James. The funeral at Chelsea Old Church is followed by cremation at Golders Green; the ashes are smuggled into America by Mrs William James and buried beside the graves of his mother and sister.

1917   (September) *The Ivory Tower* and *The Sense of the Past*, and
           (October) *The Middle Years* published (all unfinished).
1919   (March) *Within the Rim* (essays) published.

A collected edition of James's novels and stories in thirty-five volumes
under the editorship of Percy Lubbock was published in 1921–3. His
collected critical prefaces were published as *The Art of the Novel* in 1934,
The Notebooks of Henry James in 1947, and *The Complete Plays of Henry James*
in 1949.

Part I

Impressions

'Pleasure under Difficulties'*

ALICE JAMES

... I remember so distinctly the first time I was conscious of a purely intellectual process. 'Twas the summer of '56[1] which we spent in Boulogne.... We were turned into the garden to play, a sandy or rather dusty expanse with nothing in it, as I remember, but two or three scrubby apple-trees, from one of which hung a swing.... Harry was sitting in the swing and I came up and stood near by as the sun began to slant over the desolate expanse, as the dready h[ou]rs, with that endlessness which they have for infancy, passed, when Harry suddenly exclaimed: 'This might certainly be called pleasure under difficulties.' The stir of my whole being in response to the substance and exquisite, *original* form of this remark almost makes my heart beat now with the sisterly pride which was then awakened and it came to me in a flash, the higher nature of this appeal to the mind, as compared to the rudimentary solicitations which usually produced my childish explosions of laughter.

NOTE

Alice James (1848–92), sister of Henry James (whom she refers to as Harry), was the fifth and last child of Henry and Mary James. She came to England in November 1884 and lived in London and Leamington. Her invalidism seems to have been largely psychological in origin; but early in 1891 breast cancer was diagnosed, and she died on 6 March 1892. Her diary was begun on 31 May 1889 and the final entries were dictated within a few hours of her loss of consciousness (4 March 1892). Leon Edel has described it as a 'record of her sickroom world'. It reveals an extraordinary sensibility and self-awareness, and an originality and directness of style, that at times recall the poems of Emily Dickinson. Four copies were privately printed in 1894. Henry James destroyed his copy and urged that the diary should not be published, declaring himself 'terribly scared and disconcerted – I mean alarmed – by the sight of so many private names and

---

* *The Diary of Alice James*, ed. Leon Edel (London: Hart-Davis, 1965) pp. 128–9.

allusions in print'. In a letter to William James (28 May 1894) he speaks of Alice's 'extraordinary force of mind and character' and of her diary as 'heroic in its individuality, its independence – its face-to-face with the universe for-and-by herself'.

Leon Edel has said that Henry James and his sister enjoyed 'an intimate kinship that transcended ties of family, a strong emotional compatibility reaching back to their early years'. In her diary for 12 April 1891, Alice writes:

> It is unusual to see a creature like H. who with so strong, almost complete, artistic inclination, has absolutely a physical repulsion from all personal disorder. 'Tis a sad fate, though, that he should have fastened to him a being like me; and you can't exaggerate the beautiful patience with which he listens to my outpourings on *Questions* (Heaven forbid that I should ever be so base as to descend to *Subjects*) from which he is so detached, and which absorb my rawboned, relentlessly moral organisation.   (p. 192)

Elsewhere she writes of Henry's 'absolute unworldliness and inability to conceive of the base, notwithstanding his living so much in the world' (25 March 1890; p. 105), and observes that 'it is so reposeful to see him, he is so unsuggestive as to the conduct of life – the angle of one's cushions or the number of one's shawls' (13 May 1890; p. 115). On 17 June 1891 she claimed that her brother 'has embedded in his pages many pearls fallen from my lips, which he steals in the most unblushing way, saying, simply, that he knew they had been said by the family, so it did not matter' (p. 212). For further extracts from Alice James's diary, see pp. 12, 61.

1. Perhaps an error for 1857. On 27 June 1855, when Henry James was twelve years old, he and his family sailed for Europe. They landed in Liverpool on 8 July and proceeded via London to Paris and Geneva. After two months in Switzerland, they returned to London for the winter. In the early summer of 1856 they went once again to Paris, and in the summer of 1857 they made a lengthy visit to Boulogne (*Untried Years*, p. 132).

'A Very Earnest Fellow'*

WILLIAM DEAN HOWELLS

Talking of talks: young Henry James and I had a famous one last evening, two or three hours long, in which we settled the true principles of literary art. He is a very earnest fellow, and I think extremely gifted –

* *Life in Letters of William Dean Howells*, ed. Mildred Howells (New York: Doubleday, Doran, 1928) I, p. 116.

gifted enough to do better than any one has yet done toward making us a real American novel. We have in reserve from him a story for the *Atlantic*,[1] which I'm sure you'll like.

NOTE

William Dean Howells (1837–1920), American novelist and critic. He and James enjoyed a lifelong friendship, and their correspondence extends over almost fifty years. The character of Lambert Strether in *The Ambassadors* is said to be based on Howells. As assistant editor of the *Atlantic Monthly* he published some of James's early stories. Later he became, in Leon Edel's words, 'a distinguished editor and writer of fiction, and ultimately "dean" of American letters' (*Untried Years*, p. 271). The extract is taken from a letter to E. C. Stedman dated 5 December 1866.

1. 'Poor Richard', published in the *Atlantic Monthly* in June–August 1867 and reprinted in *Stories Revived* (1885).

'The American James'*

WILLIAM DEAN HOWELLS

It is not strange that I cannot recall my first meeting with Henry James, or for that matter the second or third or specifically any after meeting. It is so with every acquaintance, I suppose. All I can say is that we seemed presently to be always meeting, at his father's house and at mine, but in the kind Cambridge streets rather than those kind Cambridge houses which it seems to me I frequented more than he. We seem to have been presently always together, and always talking of methods of fiction, whether we walked the streets by day or night, or we sat together reading our stuff to each other; his stuff which we both hoped might make itself into matter for the *Atlantic Monthly*, then mostly left to my editing by my senior editor Mr Fields.[1]

I was seven years older than James, but I was much his junior in the art we both adored. Perhaps I did not yet feel my fiction definitely in me. I supposed myself a poet, and I knew myself a journalist and a traveller

* *Life in Letters of William Dean Howells*, II, pp. 397–9.

in such books as *Venetian Life* and *Italian Journeys*, and the volume of *Suburban Sketches*² where I was beginning to study our American life as I have ever since studied it. But I am distinctly aware of a walk late in the night up and down North Avenue, and of his devoting to our joint scrutiny the character of the remote branches of his family in the interest of art. They were uncles and cousins of New York origin and of that derivation which gave us their whole most interesting Celtic race. His family was settled at Albany where his grandfather was chief citizen and a foremost business man. From him branched off and down the uncles and cousins of his artistic enquiry.

Our walks were by day and by night but our sessions in my little house were twice or thrice by night a week and on Sunday were always after our simple family supper where he joined us only in spirit, for he ate nothing then or ever, except the biscuit he crumbled in his pocket and fed himself after the prescription of a famous doctor then prevalent among people of indigestion. He was a constant sufferer, tacit and explicit, and it was a form of escape from this misery for him to talk of what he was writing with the young pair whom he frequented and to read of it as far as it was written. We were of like Latin sympathies, he was inveterately and intensely French, and with the Italian use of our three or four years' life in Italy we could make him feel that we met on common ground. James could not always keep his French background back, and sometimes he wrote English that the editor easily convicted of Gallicism; but this was the helplessness of early use and habit from his life and school in France throughout boyhood.

From whatever strangeness of his French past we now joined in an American present around the airtight stove which no doubt over-heated our little parlour. I had learned to like his fiction from such American subjects as *Poor Richard*,³ but now it was such a French theme as *Gabrielle de Bergerac*⁴ which had employed his art, and which he first talked over with me and read to us by the light of our kerosene globe-lamp. We were sufficiently critical no doubt as an editorial family should be, but we richly felt the alien quality and circumstance of the tales and novels which I eagerly accepted from him, even one of a supposed humorous cast which we both grieved to find unacceptable.

I do not know how many were the nocturnal rambles which followed one another into the mild autumnal weather of the Jameses' coming to Cambridge; six months after our own settlement there. One of the aimless strolls took us to the wooded quadrangle, now long since doubtless vanished into forgotten formlessness where James resentfully identified in a much-windowed very plain mansion the house where he lodged when an unwilling student of the Harvard Law School. It is not known by whose volition he was studying law, but it was distinctly by his own that he ceased to do so, perhaps wholly unopposed by his family, but that is part of his story very dimly known to me.

Our walks by day were only in one direction and in one region. We were always going to Fresh Pond, in those days a wandering space of woods and water where people skated in winter and boated in summer.

NOTES

On Howells, see p. 5. This fragment was composed on his deathbed. In the words of Mildred Howells, the editor of his *Life in Letters* (II, p. 394),

> After Howells had written his last letter, and even after he had to be kept under drugs to deaden his pain, he was still working on two papers about Henry James, whose letters had just been published. One was an [article] on *The Letters of Henry James*, and the other, 'The American James', was an effort to say what Howells had always felt – that James was deeply and entirely American.... They are the last things Howells wrote and form the final act in a long friendship.

1. James T. Fields (1817–81), author and publisher; see also pp. 86–7.
2. Published in, respectively, 1866, 1867 and 1871.
3. See p. 5.
4. Published posthumously in 1918.

First Meeting*

EDMUND GOSSE

His welcome into English society was remarkable if we reflect that he seemed to have little to give in return for what it offered except his social adaptability, his pleasant and still formal amenity, and his admirable capacity for listening. It cannot be repeated too clearly that the Henry James of those early days had very little of the impressiveness of his later

* 'Henry James', *London Mercury*, I (1920) pp. 678–80.

manner. He went everywhere, sedately, watchfully, graciously, but never prominently. In the winter of 1878–9 it is recorded that he dined out in London 107 times, but it is highly questionable whether this amazing assiduity at the best dinner-tables will be found to have impressed itself on any Greville or Crabb Robinson who was taking notes at the time. He was strenuously living up to his standard, 'my charming little standard of wit, of grace, of good manners, of vivacity, of urbanity, of intelligence, of what makes an easy and natural style of intercourse'. He was watching the rather gross and unironic, but honest and vigorous, English upper-middle-class of that day with mingled feelings, in which curiosity and a sort of remote sympathy took a main part. At 107 London dinners he observed the ever-shifting pieces of the general kaleidoscope with tremendous acuteness, and although he thought their reds and yellows would have been improved by a slight infusion of the Florentine harmony, on the whole he was never weary of watching their evolutions. In this way the years slipped by, while he made a thousand acquaintances and a dozen durable friendships. It is a matter of pride and happiness to me that I am able to touch on one of the latter.

It is often curiously difficult for intimate friends, who have the impression in later years that they must always have known one another, to recall the occasion and the place where they first met. That was the case with Henry James and me. Several times we languidly tried to recover those particulars, but without success. I think, however, that it was at some dinner-party that we first met, and as the incident is dubiously connected with the publication of the *Hawthorne* in 1879, and with Mr (now Lord) Morley,[1] whom we both frequently saw at that epoch, I am pretty sure that the event took place early in 1880. The acquaintance, however, did not 'ripen', as people say, until the summer of 1882, when in connection with an article on the drawings of George du Maurier, which I was anxious Henry James should write – having heard him express himself with high enthusiasm regarding these works of art – he invited me to go to see him and to talk over the project. I found him, one sunshiny afternoon, in his lodgings on the first floor of No. 3 Bolton Street, at the Piccadilly end of the street, where the houses look askew into Green Park. Here he had been living ever since he came over from France in 1876, and the situation was eminently characteristic of the impassioned student of London life and haunter of London society which he had now become.

Stretched on the sofa and apologising for not rising to greet me, his appearance gave me a little shock, for I had not thought of him as an invalid. He hurriedly and rather evasively declared that he was not that, but that a muscular weakness of his spine obliged him, as he said, 'to assume the horizontal posture' during some hours of every day in order to bear the almost unbroken routine of evening engagements. I think that this weakness gradually passed away, but certainly for many years it handicapped his activity. I recall his appearance, seen then for the first time by daylight; there was something shadowy about it, the face framed in dark brown hair cut short in the Paris fashion, and in equally dark beard, rather loose and 'fluffy'. He was in deep mourning, his mother having died five or six months earlier, and he himself having but recently returned from a melancholy visit to America, where he had unwillingly left his father, who seemed far from well. His manner was grave, extremely courteous, but a little formal and frightened, which seemed strange in a man living in constant communication with the world. Our business regarding du Maurier was soon concluded, and James talked with increasing ease, but always with a punctilious hesitancy, about Paris, where he seemed, to my dazzlement, to know even a larger number of persons of distinction than he did in London.

He promised, before I left, to return my visit, but news of the alarming illness of his father called him suddenly to America. He wrote to me from Boston in April 1883, but he did not return to London until the autumn that year. Our intercourse was then resumed, and, immediately, on the familiar footing which it preserved, without an hour's abatement, until the sad moment of his fatal illness. When he returned to Bolton Street – this was in August 1883 – he had broken all the ties which held him to residence in America, a country which, as it turned out, he was not destined to revisit for more than twenty years. By this means Henry James became a homeless man in a peculiar sense, for he continued to be looked upon as a foreigner in London, while he seemed to have lost citizenship in the United States. It was a little later than this that that somewhat acidulated patriot, Colonel Higginson, in reply to some one who said that Henry James was a cosmopolitan, remarked, 'Hardly! for a cosmopolitan is at home even in his own country!' This condition made James, although superficially gregarious, essentially isolated, and though his books were numerous and were greatly admired, they were tacitly ignored alike in summaries of English and of American current literature. There was no escape from this dilemma. Henry James was equally determined not to lay down his American birthright and not to reside in America. Every year of his exile, therefore, emphasised the fact of his separation from all other Anglo-Saxons, and he endured, in the world of letters, the singular fate of being a man without a country.

NOTE

Edmund Gosse (1849–1928), author and critic, is now best remembered for his autobiographical book *Father and Son* (1907). His many literary friendships included Swinburne, Stevenson and Hardy. Gosse and James met in the mid-eighties; they remained friends for the rest of James's life and exchanged many letters.

1. John Morley (1838–1923), author and politician, was editor of the popular series of short biographical studies, English Men of Letters, to which James contributed a life of Hawthorne.

A Child's View of Henry James*

COMPTON MACKENZIE

... that first far away meeting with Henry James remains vivid. The very day can be fixed because Henry James himself noted it in the space for his birthday signature on 15 April. It was 5 May 1890. Henry James was just forty-seven: I was a few weeks over seven.

As my father and I walked along by Kensington Gardens I was told how he when a boy at school had met Thackeray walking along this same stretch of pavement with *his* father and how the great man had tipped him handsomely. Not yet being at school myself, I did not regard middle-aged gentlemen as milch cows and therefore did not cross the road to De Vere Gardens with the smallest expectations from Henry James. At that date he wore a beard, and I remember the almost ritualistic courtesy of his welcome to what he once called his 'chaste and secluded Kensington quatrième ... flooded with light like a photographer's studio'. He was, it might have seemed, absurdly solicitous for the comfort of the seven-year-old visitor before he immersed himself with its father in the mysterious deeps of the theatre. I was warned by the paternal finger on the paternal lips not to interrupt the colloquy. Not that I was remotely planning such a sacrilege. My attention was

* 'Henry James', *Life and Letters Today*, XXXIX (December 1943) pp. 147–9.

preoccupied by the variety of desks of different heights and by a kind of day-bed along the wall to which a reading-desk was attached. Finally I was bidden to produce my birthday book, and I had the gratification of seeing Henry James take it to the tallest and to me the most puzzling desk in a corner beside the windows and inscribe his name, standing. That anybody should stand at a desk to write cut charply for my childish fancy a difference between authors and the rest of mankind.

Probably in the course of this visit to 34 De Vere Gardens it was more or less settled that my father should produce James's dramatised version of his novel *The American*.[1] The author would be writing to his sister from Venice two months later to say how 'ravished' he was by her letter after reading the play, which was to be produced first in the provinces and next year in London. He would be congratulating himself upon the technical experience he had gained from writing a play that would act in 'to a minute, including entr'actes, 2 hours and $\frac{3}{4}$'. Here Henry James was premature. In the autumn he went to Sheffield to read the play before it was put into rehearsal to the company that would perform it. The reading began at eleven o'clock and finished at a quarter to three.

'Well?' the author asked anxiously, when he and the actor–manager came out of the stage-door to take a short walk before dining together at half-past three, 'What was your impression, Compton?'

'It's too long,' said my father.

'Too long?' James repeated in courteous but distressed amazement.

'It took you three hours and three-quarters to read it and there are three intervals to allow for.'

'What shall we do?'

'We shall have to cut it.'

Henry James stopped dead and gazed at my father in agony.

'Cut it?' he gasped. 'Did you say "cut it"? But when we discussed the play you did not suggest it was too long.'

'No, it was not too long then. You've added at least forty pages to the script.'

'But here and there additions and modifications were necessary', the author insisted.

Later on that afternoon my mother was able to prevail on Henry James to allow her to make suggestions for cuts, and that led to a formidable correspondence between them, much of it carried on by James in very long and elaborate telegrams offering to sacrifice a couple of 'that's' on one page. Fifteen years earlier Tennyson had handed over *Queen Mary* to be cut by my grandmother for production on the stage. I have a letter to her in which the poet's depression is revealed in a postscript; 'Do you think *all* the changes good?'

On the evening of that day in Sheffield when Henry James read *The American* to the company he saw a performance of *The School for Scandal*. After the curtain had fallen he went round to my father's dressing-room. For some minutes James sat in a contemplative silence. At last my father, in the way of the actor–manager, asked him how he had enjoyed Sheridan's comedy.

'A curious old play', said Henry James slowly. 'A very curious old play', he repeated in a tone that revealed his astonishment that such a play could still be put on the stage. And that was the only comment he made.

NOTE

Compton (later Sir Compton) Mackenzie (1883–1972), novelist and autobiographer; son of the actor Edward Compton, who produced and appeared in Henry James's first play, a dramatisation of *The American* (see p. 61). Mackenzie's mother, the actress Virginia Bateman, also had a part in the play. His novel *Carnival* (1912) was a considerable success. When the first volume of his *Sinister Street* appeared in 1913, James praised it extravagantly; but he was disappointed by the second volume (1914). James wrote numerous letters to Mackenzie and refers to him in his article 'The Younger Generation', published in *The Times Literary Supplement* on 19 March and 2 April 1914 and revised and enlarged for its appearance in *Notes on Novelists* (1914).

1. See above. The text is given in *The Complete Plays of Henry James*, ed. Leon Edel (New York: Lippincott, 1949).

'The Demoralisation of English Society'*

ALICE JAMES

Harry came in the other day quite sickened from a conversation he had been listening to which he said gave him a stronger impression of the demoralisation of English society than anything he had ever heard. He

* *The Diary of Alice James*, pp. 153–4.

had been calling upon a lady whom he knows very well and who is very well connected; two gentlemen were there, one young, the other old; one of them asked about one of the sons who has just failed in an exam for one of the services, when she said he had just had an offer of a place his opinion of which she would like to have. Pulitzer,[1] the ex-editor of the *New York World*, had applied to the British embassy in Paris to recommend him a young man of good family to act as his secretary, write his letters, etc., but chiefly to be socially useful in attracting people to the house – to act, in short, evidently, as a decoy duck to Pulitzer's gilded salons. A young man rejoicing in the name of Claude Ponsonby had fulfilled the functions for three years, and had just been married to an American, Pulitzer having given him a 'dot' of £30,000 and it was presumable that his successor would fare equally well. The Englishmen both thought it would be 'a jolly life'. She then turned and asked H. what he thought – 'I would rather sweep the dirtiest crossing in London!' At which rejoinder staring amazement! H. asked if she knew Pulitzer's history, that he had made his money editing the vulgarest conceivable newspaper, oh, yes, she knew all about him and her only anxiety was that the son who was a complete failure might fail in getting the enviable berth. The snobling, it appears, has a strong taste for medicine but thinks it a social disgrace to be a doctor, conceiving a social tout to a Pulitzer to be a nobler form of man.

In coming home, H. saw tossing about among a lot of photos of actresses and ballet girls in a shop, a photo of the beautiful Lady Helen Duncombe – who has just married some one, lying out on a chair or sofa with her arms crossed over her head – to this have all the fine heredities brought the present generation of the aristocracy – how they are crumbling and mouldering from within! Harry said he entirely disbelieved the story of the £30,000 marriage present. I remember H. telling me some years ago that Pulitzer came to him and asked him to write some stories for the *New York World*, that the only essential quality for them was that they mustn't have 'anything literary' about them.

NOTE

On Alice James, see p. 3. The extract is dated 9 November 1890; Alice was at this time living in London.

1. Joseph Pulitzer (1847–1911), American newspaper publisher.

'Remarkably Unremarkable'*

W. GRAHAM ROBERTSON

The Henry James of those days was strangely unlike the remarkable-looking man of almost twenty years later, who was ... painted by Sargent.[1]

In the nineties he was in appearance almost remarkably unremarkable; his face might have been anybody's face; it was as though, when looking round for a face, he had been able to find nothing to his taste and had been obliged to put up with a ready-made 'stock' article until something more suitable could be made to order expressly for him.

This special and only genuine Henry James's face was not 'delivered' until he was a comparatively old man, so that for the greater part of his life he went about in disguise.

My mother, who was devoted to his works, used to be especially annoyed by this elusive personality.

'I always want so much to talk with him,' she complained, 'yet when I meet him I never can remember who he is.'

Perhaps to make up for this indistinguishable presence he cultivated impressiveness of manner and great preciosity of speech.

He had a way of leaving a dinner-party early with an air of preoccupation that was very intriguing.

'He always does it', untruthfully exclaimed a deserted and slightly piqued hostess. 'It is to convey the suggestion that he has an appointment with a Russian princess.'

In later life both the impressive manner and fastidious speech became intensified: what he said was always interesting, but he took so long to say it that one felt a growing conviction that he was not for a moment, but for all time. With him it was a moral obligation to find the *mot juste*, and if it had got mislaid or was far to seek, the world had to stand still until it turned up.

Sometimes when it arrived it was delightfully unexpected. I remember

* *Time Was* (London: Hamish Hamilton, 1931) pp. 238–9.

in later years walking with him round my little Surrey garden and manoeuvring him to a spot where a rather wonderful view suddenly revealed itself.

'My dear boy', exclaimed Henry James, grasping my arm. 'How – er – how –' I waited breathless: the *mot juste* was on its way; at least I should hear the perfect and final summing up of my countryside's loveliness. 'How – er – how –' still said Mr James, until at long last the golden sentence sprang complete from his lips. 'My dear boy, how awfully jolly!'

I also recall his telling of a tale about an American business man who had bought a large picture.

'And when he got it home,' continued Mr James, 'he did not know what – er – what –'

'What to do with it', prompted some impatient and irreverent person.

Henry James silently rejected the suggestion. 'He did not know what – er – what – well, in point of fact, the *hell* to do with it.'

NOTE

W. Graham Robertson (1866–1948) was an author, illustrator and dramatist.

1. John Singer Sargent (1856–1925), portrait painter, was born in Italy of an American father. James met him in Paris in 1884 and persuaded him to go to London; he settled there and became a Royal Academician in 1897. On the portrait of James painted by Sargent to commemorate his seventieth birthday, see p. 145.

'Divinely Interesting'*

WILLIAM DEAN HOWELLS

I had two days in London, and saw James continuously and exclusively. I never saw him more divinely interesting, and he told me I had been useful to him, in giving him a new business perspective. He seemed to have got needlessly but deeply discouraged, and I was able to reassure him of his public here.

* *Life in Letters of William Dean Howells*, II, p. 83.

NOTE

On Howells, see p. 5. The extract is from a letter to Charles Eliot Norton dated 27 December 1897.

A Non-literary Intimacy*

FORD MADOX FORD

I think I will, after reflection, lay claim to a very considerable degree of intimacy with Henry James. It was a winter, and a wholly non-literary intimacy. That is to say, during the summers we saw little of each other. He had his friends and I mine. He was too often expecting 'my friend Lady Maude', or some orthodox critic to tea and I, modern poets whom he could not abide. Occasionally, even during the summer, he would send from Rye to Winchelsea, a distance of two miles, telegrams such as the following which I transcribe:

'To FORD MADOX HUEFFER, Esq.,
'The Bungalow, Winchelsea, near Rye, Sussex.
'May I bring four American ladies, of whom one a priest, to tea to-day?
'Yours sincerely, HENRY JAMES.'

And he would come.

But, in the winters, when London visitors were scarce, he would come to tea every other day with almost exact regularity, and I would walk back with him to Rye. On the alternate days I would have tea with him and he would walk back to Winchelsea, in all weathers, across the wind-swept marshes. That was his daily, four miles, constitutional.

But it was, as I have said, an almost purely non-literary intimacy. I could, I think, put down on one page all that he ever said to me of books – and, although I used, out of respect, to send him an occasional book of

* *Thus to Revisit: Some Reminiscences* (London: Chapman & Hall, 1921) pp. 113–17, 118–19, 121–2, 123–5.

my own on publication, and he an occasional book of his to me, he never said a word to me about my writings and I do not remember ever having done more than thank him in letters for his volume of the moment. I remember his saying of *Romance*[1] that it was an immense English Plum Cake which he kept at his bedside for a fortnight and of which he ate a nightly slice.

He would, if he never talked of books, frequently talk of the personalities of their writers – not infrequently in terms of shuddering at their social excesses, much as he shuddered at contact with Crane.[2] He expressed intense dislike for Flaubert who 'opened his own door in his dressing-gown'[3] and he related, not infrequently, unrepeatable stories of the ménages of Maupassant[4] – but he much preferred Maupassant to 'poor dear old Flaubert'. Of Turgenev's[5] appearance, personality and habits he would talk with great tendernesses of expression – he called him nearly always 'the beautiful Russian genius', and would tell stories of Turgenev's charming attentions to his peasant mistresses. He liked, in fact, persons who were suave when you met them – and I daresay that his preference of that sort coloured his literary tastes. He preferred Maupassant to Flaubert because Maupassant was *homme du monde* – or at any rate had *femmes du monde* for his mistresses; and he preferred Turgenev to either because Turgenev was a quiet aristocrat and invalid of the German Bathing Towns, to the finger tips. And he liked – he used to say so – people who treated him with deep respect.

Flaubert he hated with a lasting, deep rancour. Flaubert had once abused him unmercifully – over a point in the style of Prosper Mérimée,[6] of all people in the world. You may read about it in the *Correspondence* of Flaubert, and James himself referred to the occasion several times. It seemed to make it all the worse that, just before the outbreak, Flaubert should have opened the front door of his flat to Turgenev and James, in his dressing-gown.

Myself, I suppose he must have liked, because I treated him with deep respect, had a low voice – appeared, in short, *a jeune homme modeste*. Occasionally he would burst out at me with furious irritation – as if I had been a stupid nephew. This would be particularly the case if I ventured to have any opinions about the United States – which, at that date, I had visited much more lately than he had. I remember one occasion very vividly – the place, beside one of the patches of thorn on the Rye road, and his aspect, the brown face with the dark eyes rolling in the whites, the compact, strong figure, the stick raised so as to be dug violently into the road. He had been talking two days before of the provincialism of Washington in the sixties. He said that when one descended the steps of the Capitol in those days *on trébuchait sur des vaches* – one stumbled over cows, as if on a village green. Two days later, I don't know why – I happened to return to the subject of the provincialism of Washington in the sixties. He stopped as if I had hit him and, with the coldly infuriated tone of a country squire whose patriotism has been outraged, exclaimed:

'Don't talk such *damnable* nonsense!' He really shouted these words with a male fury. And when, slightly outraged myself I returned to the charge with his own *on trébuchait sur des vaches*, he exclaimed: 'I should not have thought you would have wanted to display such ignorance', and hurried off along the road....

When I first knew him you could have imagined no oak more firmly planted in European soil. But, little by little, when he talked about America there would come into his tones a slight tremulousness that grew with the months. I remember, once he went to see some friends – Mrs and Miss Lafarge,[7] I think – off to New York from Tilbury Dock. He came back singularly excited, bringing out a great many unusually uncompleted sentences. He had gone over the liner: 'And once aboard the lugger ... And if ... Say a toothbrush ... And circular notes ... And something for the night ... And if ... By Jove, I might have ...' All this with a sort of diffident shamefacedness....

It has always seemed to me inscrutable that he should have been so frequently damned for his depicting only one phase of life; as if it were his fault that he was not also Mr Conrad, to write of the sea, or Crane, to project the life of the New York slums. The Old Man knew consummately one form of life; to that he restricted himself. I have heard him talk with extreme exactness and insight of the life of the poor – at any rate of the agricultural poor, for I do not remember ever to have heard him discuss industrialism. But he knew that he did not know enough to treat of farm-labourers in his writing. So that, mostly, when he discoursed of these matters he put his observations in the form of questions: 'Didn't I agree to this?' 'Hadn't I found that?'

But indeed, although I have lived amongst agricultural labourers a good deal at one time or another, I would cheerfully acknowledge that his knowledge – at any rate of their psychologies – had a great deal more insight than my own. He had such an extraordinary gift for observing minutiæ – and a gift still more extraordinary for making people talk. I have heard the secretary of a golf-club, a dour silent man who never addressed five words to myself though I was one of his members, talk for twenty minutes to the Master about a new bunker that he was thinking of making at the fourteenth hole. And James had never touched a niblick in his life. It was the same with market-women, tram-conductors, shipbuilders' labourers, auctioneers. I have stood by and heard them talk to him for hours. Indeed, I am fairly certain that he once had a murder confessed to him. But he needed to stand on extraordinarily firm ground before he would think that he knew a world. And what he knew he rendered, along with its amenities, its gentlefolkishness, its pettinesses, its hypocrisies, its make-believes. He gives you an immense – and an increasingly tragic – picture of a Leisured Society that is fairly unavailing, materialist, emasculated – and doomed. No one was more aware of all that than he. . . .

I will not say that loveableness was the predominating feature of the Old Man: he was too intent on his own particular aims to be lavishly sentimental over surrounding humanity. And his was not a character painted in the flat, in watercolour, like the caricatures of Rowlandson. For some protective reason or other, just as Shelley used to call himself the Atheist, he loved to appear in the character of a sort of Mr Pickwick – with the rather superficial benevolences, and the mannerisms of which he was perfectly aware. But below that protective mask was undoubtedly a plane of nervous cruelty. I have heard him be – to simple and quite unpretentious people – more diabolically blighting than it was quite decent for a man to be – for he was always an artist in expression. And it needed a certain fortitude when, the studied benevolence and the chuckling, savouring, enjoyment of words, disappearing suddenly from his personality, his dark eyes rolled in their whites and he spoke very brutal and direct English. He chose in fact to appear as Henrietta Maria – but he could be atrocious to those who behaved as if they took him at that valuation.

And there was yet a third depth – a depth of religious, of mystical, benevolence such as you find just now and again in the stories that he 'wanted' to write – in the *Great Good Places*[8]. . . . His practical benevolences were innumerable, astonishing – and indefatigable. To do a kindness when a sick cat or dog of the human race *had* 'got through' to his mind as needing assistance he would exhibit all the extraordinary ingenuities that are displayed in his most involved sentences. When 'poor dear Stevie'[9] at Brede fell sick of his last, protracted illness, the personal concern that James showed was almost fantastic. He turned his days into long debates over this or that benevolence – and he lay all night awake fearing that he might have contemplated something that might wound the feelings or appear patronising to the sick boy. He would run the gamut of grapes, public subscriptions, cheques. He cabled to New York for sweet-corn and soft-shelled crabs for fear the boy might long for home-food. And, when they came he threw them away – for fear they should make him more home-sick! . . .

I may as well now confess that in drawing Henry VIII in one of my own novels[10] I was rendering the Master in externals – and mighty life-like the Press of those days found the portrait to be. . . . I dare say, anyhow, that he took me to be a journalist of a gentle disposition, too languid to interrupt him. Once, after I had sent him one of my volumes of poems, he just mentioned the name of the book, raised both his hands over his head, let them slowly down again, made an extraordinary, quick grimace, and shook with an immense internal joke. . . . Shortly afterwards he began to poke fun at Swinburne.

In revenge, constantly and with every appearance of according weight to my opinions, though he seldom waited for an answer, he would consult me about practical matters – investments now and then, agreements once or twice – and, finally, unceasingly as to his fantastic domestic arrangements. He had at one stage portentous but increasingly unsatisfactory servants of whom, in his kindness of heart, he would not get rid until their conduct became the talk of the Antient Town of Rye.

So, one day he came over to Winchelsea to ask me if I thought a Lady Help would be a desirable feature in an eminent bachelor's establishment. . . . Going as we seemed eternally in those days to be doing, down Winchelsea Hill under the Strand Gate, he said:

'H . . . , you seem worried!' I said that I was worried. I don't know how he knew. But he knew everything.

Ellen Terry[11] waved her gracious hand from the old garden above the tower; the collar of Maximilian the dachshund called for adjustment. He began another interminable, refining, sentence – about housemaids and their locutions. It lasted us to the bridge at the western foot of Rye.

In Rye High Street he exclaimed – he was extraordinarily flustered:

'I perceive a compatriot. Let us go into this shop!' And he bolted into a fruiterer's. He came out holding an orange and, eventually, throwing it into the air in an ecstasy of nervousness and stuttering like a schoolboy:

'If it's money H . . .' he brought out. 'Mon sac n'est pas grand. . . . Mais puisez dans mon sac!'

I explained that it was not about money that I was worried, but about the 'form' of a book I was writing. His mute agony was a painful thing to see. He became much more appalled, but much less nervous. At last he made the great sacrifice:

'Well, then,' he said, 'I'm supposed to be . . . Um, um . . . There's Mary . . . Mrs Ward[12] . . . does me the honour . . . I'm supposed to know . . . In short: why not let me look at the manuscript!'

I had the decency not to take up his time with it. . . . Les beaux jours quand on était bien modeste! And how much I regret that I did not.

The last time I saw him was, accidentally, in August of 1915 – on the fourteenth of that month, in St James's Park. He said:

'Tu vas te battre pour le sol sacré de Mme de Stael!'

I suppose it was characteristic that he should say 'de Mme de Stael' – and not of Stendhal, or even of George Sand! He added – and how sincerely and with what passion – putting one hand on his chest and just bowing, that he loved and had loved France as he had never loved a woman!

NOTES

Ford Madox Ford (1873–1939), formerly Ford Madox Hueffer, novelist and critic, wrote several volumes of reminiscences in which the same material is often repeated with variations. Most of the material in the above extract can also be found in *Return to Yesterday* (New York: Liveright, 1932) pp. 205–13, and some of it in *Mightier than the Sword* (London: Allen & Unwin, 1938), which has a chapter devoted to James. James met Hueffer (as he then was) in 1896; later Hueffer lived in a bungalow at Winchelsea, near Rye, and they met frequently. As a memoirist Ford is unreliable.

1. Novel, published in 1903, in which Hueffer collaborated with Joseph Conrad.

2. Stephen Crane (1871–1900), American novelist. James met him in 1898; early in 1899 Crane went to live at Brede, Sussex, only a few miles from Rye, and paid a number of visits to Lamb House. Crane's wife Cora had formerly kept a brothel in Jacksonville, Florida.

3. The episode is described more fully in *Mightier than the Sword*:

Flaubert had ... once been rude to the young James. That James never mentioned. But he had subsequently received James and Turgenev in his dressing-gown. It was not, of course, a dressing-gown, but a working garment – a sort of long, loose coat without revers – called a *chandail*. And if a French man of letters received you in his *chandail*, he considered it a sort of showing honour, as if he had admitted you into his working intimacy. But James never forgave that.... Flaubert for ever afterwards was for him the man who worked, who thought, who received, who lived – and perhaps went to heaven in his dressing-gown! (p. 30)

4. Guy de Maupassant (1850–93), French novelist and short story writer; James had met him during his residence in Paris.

5. Ivan Sergievich Turgenev (1818–83), Russian novelist; James had met him in Paris.

6. Prosper Mérimée (1803–70), French novelist and dramatist.

7. Mrs John Lafarge was an old friend of James's from his American years. The episode referred to took place in November 1903.

8. The reference is to James's story 'The Great Good Place', first published in 1900.

9. See note 2 above.

10. The reference is to Hueffer's historical trilogy *The Fifth Queen* (1906–8).

11. Ellen Terry (1847–1928), English actress celebrated for her Shakespearean roles and remembered for her association with Henry Irving and G. B. Shaw. She had been in the audience at the first night of *Guy Domville*, and James called on her by invitation on 5 February 1895. See also p. 53.

12. Mrs Humphry Ward: see p. 42.

James's Friendships*

HUGH WALPOLE

Immature though I was I perceived instantly his inevitable loneliness. He was lonely in the first place because, an American, he was never really at home in Europe. Nor was he at home in America for when he was there he longed for the age, the quiet, the sophistications of Europe.

He was lonely in the second place because he was a spectator of life. He was a spectator because his American ancestry planted a reticent Puritanism in his temperament and this was for ever at war with his intellectual curiosity.

Sexually also he had suffered some frustration. What that frustration was I never knew but I remember his telling me how he had once in his youth in a foreign town watched a whole night in pouring rain for the appearance of a figure at a window. 'That was the end . . .' he said, and broke off.

His passion for his friends – Lucy Clifford,[1] Edith Wharton,[2] Jocelyn Persse,[3] Mrs Prothero,[4] among others – was the intense longing of a lonely man. It was most unselfish and noble. His love for his own relations, his brother William, his nephew, had a real pathos for although they beautifully returned it they could never be so deeply absorbed in him as he was in them. I went once to Brown's Hotel to say goodbye to him before his departure for America with William James who was very ill. While I was with him a message came and he hurried away. I waited and waited but no one came, so at last I started

* 'Henry James: a Reminiscence', *Horizon*, I (February 1940) pp. 76–80.

downstairs. I passed an open bedroom door and saw William lying on the floor and Henry standing over him. As I hurried down I caught an expression of misery and despair on Henry's face that I shall never forget.

It has become, in these fierce and bitter days, suspicious to speak of nobility of character but it must be risked when one speaks of Henry James. He had in relation with his friends so many things to put up with! First of all our intellects. Edith Wharton alone seemed to satisfy him intellectually and that I always thought odd for, with the exception of *Ethan Frome* I always considered her, and consider her still, a flashy, superficial novelist. But James was never a good critic of contemporary writers. 'Poor, poor Conrad!' he would say. And he wrote of D. H. Lawrence 'trailing in the dusty rear' in those famous *Times* articles. He could see little in the novels of E. M. Forster. Wells and Bennett were to him intolerably diffuse.

He did, quite naturally, wonder why novelists in general paid so little attention to form, did not consider more seriously their 'subjects', and so on. All this is, of course, generally known. What is *not* so generally known is that the failure of his own Collected Edition⁵ struck him a blow from which he never properly recovered.

The night when the gallery booed him at the first performance of *Guy Domville* and the days when he realised that the Collected Edition over which he had worked for years, rewriting the earlier novels, composing the marvellous Prefaces, was not only not selling but was also not reviewed – these were catastrophes for him. He was as little vain and conceited as any man, but his art was something that had a value and importance altogether outside himself and his own popularity.

Just as Wells hoped that, if he kept on long enough, human beings would learn some wisdom before it was too late, so James hoped, that if *he* kept on long enough, writers would learn something of the sacrifice and service and discipline that Art demanded. But of course no one learned anything: it has needed something very much more terrible than Wells's Encyclopædia and James's cadences to bring about a realisation. . . .

So James fell back on his friends. I soon began to wonder at the contrast between the simplicity of his heart and the complexity of his brain. I knew him only after he had shaved his beard, and Sargent's portrait in the National Portrait Gallery presents him exactly as he was except when in the company of his close friends. At parties and places where people gathered together he was as ceremonial as an Oriental and many people found it very tiresome to stand at attention and wait for the long unrolling of the sentences and think of something to say in reply that was not completely idiotic. But alone with the people he loved, his humour was over all and his tenderness beneficent.

He could not do too much for his friends, could not be too close to them, could not hear too many details of their daily lives. It mattered nothing to him if their tastes were not his if he loved them. Jocelyn Persse, for example, liked horses rather than the Arts and pretended none other, but Henry was never happier than when he was in Jocelyn's company.

My enthusiasms often exasperated him and once he was really angry, with a ferocity, over some would-be critical article of mine but he accepted me for better or worse and protected me often enough against the ill humours and scorns of others.

I look back to one special case of protection that for me illuminates the whole distant scene with a nostalgic light. Some ten years ago I described it in a small privately printed book[6] and now, writing in a second war, the figures are yet more distantly removed, more ghostly but, for myself, more real.

It began with Henry James's seventieth birthday. His friends agreed to give him a replica of the Golden Bowl and his portrait painted by Sargent. A letter must be sent out asking for subscriptions. Edmund Gosse, as James's oldest literary friend, I as his youngest, were deputed to write and despatch this letter.

So soon as I heard of this I implored to be spared. I loved Gosse and was terrified of him. I was sure, in my heart, that I would make a mistake and then that cold, bitter anger would slay me – and I passionately did not want to be slain!

Henry James calmed my fears. He assured me that all would be well. He himself would see to it. So, after a beautiful letter had been composed by Gosse and a list of grand and memorable names compiled, I went down to the printers in the City to arrange for the printing and despatch. Henry James accompanied me 'so that nothing might be wrong'.

Two days later I dined alone with Maurice Hewlett.[7] For one reason or another he did not at that time care for Gosse. He met me in the hall. His sardonic eye flashing, his little 'goatee' pirouetting with pleasure on his elegant chin, he said, as he took my hand: 'Dear Hugh, I knew that you were fond of me. But I did *not* know until this morning that Gosse was. In fact I thought the contrary. I have, however, received so affectionate a letter from Gosse and yourself that I am flattered and proud.' My heart sank. Something dreadful had occurred. 'For God's sake tell me', I murmured.

With delight he showed me the letter. James and I had forgotten altogether to fill in the names of those to whom the letter was sent. The letter, therefore began: 'Dear' and ended: 'We are, Dear, yours sincerely, Edmund Gosse, Hugh Walpole.' And this to people as dignified, as unassailably great as John Morley and Mrs Humphry Ward! Oh yes, Gosse was angry! I have his letter still.

But the real point of it is that Henry James took the blame entirely upon himself and chose the reception day for the subscribers at Sargent's studio to explain the facts.

He stood beside the portrait and, as each person approached, explained that it had been *his* fault and neither Gosse's nor mine that the names had been omitted. And his explanations took a very long time. And the queue grew ever longer and longer. And I stood for hours blushing and confused. It was an amazing scene but a beautiful one.

Time we are told is no longer Time. And so, at this moment, as I write, Henry, in his brown buff waistcoat, his dark elegant clothes, is standing beside his portrait, courteous, anxious, explanatory, helping a young friend, apologising for a breach in good manners that he had not himself committed.

NOTES

Hugh Walpole (1884–1941), English novelist, was on the threshold of his literary career when he met James in February 1909. James became deeply attached to him, and they met frequently in London and Rye. In his diary for 1909, after noting that he had received a letter from James, A. C. Benson (see p. 89) wrote: 'Henry James has formed a romantic friendship with Hugh Walpole, very good and happy for both, I expect'; shortly afterwards, commenting on a conversation he had had with Walpole, Benson wrote: 'it *must* be very surprising to have Henry James fall in love with you'.

1. Lucy Clifford was the wife of a well-known mathematician and philosopher; under her married name (Mrs W. K. Clifford) she published novels. She died in 1929.

2. See p. 27.

3. Dudley Jocelyn Persse was a young Anglo-Irish man-about-town and a nephew of Lady Gregory. James met him on 7 July 1903 at the Great Central Hotel, where they were fellow-guests at Sidney Colvin's wedding celebration. They quickly became close friends: on James's side it was (in Leon Edel's phrase) 'a case of love at first sight', and he wrote many letters to Persse.

4. Fanny Prothero (born Mary Frances Butcher) was the wife of George (later Sir George) Prothero (1848–1922), historian, who taught at Cambridge (1875–94), was Professor of Modern History at Edinburgh (1894–9), and edited the *Quarterly Review* (1899–1922). Their country home was Dial Cottage, Rye;

they became friends as well as neighbours of James and he corresponded with her.

5. The New York Edition (1907–9).
6. *The Apple Trees* (London: Golden Cockerell Press, 1932).
7. Maurice Hewlett (1861–1923), novelist, poet and essayist.

James and 'the Conformities'*

EDITH WHARTON

The Henry James of the early meetings was the bearded Penseroso of Sargent's delicate drawing,[1] soberly fastidious in dress and manner, cut on the approved pattern of the *homme du monde* of the eighties; whereas by the time we got to know each other well the compact upright figure had expanded to a rolling and voluminous outline, and the elegance of dress given way to the dictates of comfort, while a clean shave had revealed in all its sculptural beauty the noble Roman mask and the big dramatic mouth. The change typified something deep beneath the surface. In the interval two things had happened: Henry James had taken the measure of the fashionable society which in youth had subjugated his imagination, as it had Balzac's, and was later to subjugate Proust's, and had fled from it to live in the country, carrying with him all the loot his adventure could yield; and in his new solitude he had come to grips with his genius. Exquisite as the early novels are – and in point of perfection probably none can touch *The Portrait of a Lady* – yet measured by what was to come Henry James, when he wrote them, had but skimmed the surface of life and of his art. Even the man who wrote, in *The Portrait of a Lady*, the chapter in which Isabel broods over her fate at night by the fire,[2] was far from the man in whom was already ripening that greater night-piece, the picture of Maggie looking in from the terrace at Fawns at the four bridge-players,[3] and renouncing her vengeance as 'nothing nearer to experience than a wild eastern caravan, looming into view with crude colours in the sun, fierce pipes in the air, high spears against the sky . . .

* *A Backward Glance* (New York: Appleton-Century, 1934) pp. 173–5.

but turning off short before it reached her and plunging into other defiles'.

But though he had found his genius and broken away from the social routine, he never emancipated himself in small matters from the conformities. Though he now affected to humour the lumbering frame whose physical ease must be considered first, he remained spasmodically fastidious about his dress, and about other trifling social observances, and once when he was motoring with us in France in 1907, and suddenly made up his mind (at Poitiers, of all places!) that he must then and there buy a new hat, almost insuperable difficulties attended its selection. It was not until he had announced his despair of ever making the hatter understand 'that what he wanted was a hat like everybody else's', and I had rather impatiently suggested his asking for a head-covering *'pour l'homme moyen sensuel'*, that the joke broke through his indecisions, and to a rich accompaniment of chuckles the hat was bought.

Still more particular about his figure than his dress, he resented any suggestion that his silhouette had lost firmness and acquired volume; and once, when my friend Jacques-Emile Blanche[4] was doing the fine seated profile portrait which is the only one that renders him *as he really was*, he privately implored me to suggest to Blanche 'not to lay such stress on the resemblance to Daniel Lambert'.[5]

NOTES

Edith Wharton (1862–1937), American novelist. Her husband, Edward Wharton, was a wealthy Boston banker; they were divorced in 1913. From 1907 she lived mainly in Paris. Her first novel, *The Touchstone*, appeared in 1900. Her fiction depicts upper-class New York society and is deeply influenced by James, whom she met in December 1903. When he visited America, James stayed at her house, The Mount, at Lenox, Massachusetts.

1. Sargent (see p. 15) executed a pencil sketch of James on 10 September 1886. It is reproduced in *The Middle Years* (London: Collins, 1917) opposite p. 289. Edith Wharton saw James on three occasions in the 1880s and early 1890s, but was not introduced to him until later.

2. *The Portrait of a Lady*, Chapter 42.

3. *The Golden Bowl*, Book Fifth, Chapter 2.

4. Blanche, a popular French portrait-painter, published *Portraits of a Lifetime* (1937).

5. Celebrated fat man, exhibited *c.* 1800.

'The Strange Alchemy of his Genius'*

ELLA HEPWORTH DIXON

When I look back, it seems to me that Henry James was the most profoundly sad-looking man I have ever seen, not even excepting certain members of the house of Rothschild. His eyes were not only age-old and world-weary, as are those of cultured Jews, but they had vision – and one did not like to think of what they saw. It is true that Henry James had plenty of sardonic humour, but he too often used it at the expense of his friends and protégés. It was always a mystery to me how the writer who gave the world that exquisite story, *An Altar of Friendship*,[1] could be so biting (though always humorous) about the people he dined with, entertained, and 'protected' in a literary sense. It was impossible not to like him, but one was continually startled at what he had to say about his contemporaries and juniors. At one time I used to meet him at certain famous 'dinners of eight', given by a woman of many graces and achievements, who easily got 'all London' round her.

One day I asked him why he no longer dined with Lady X. 'I find it more and more difficult, more and more difficult' (Henry James could not say a sentence without repeating himself) 'to put up with the second-rate', which was rather hard on our mutual hostess, who had justly made a name by her dinner-parties.

At houses where he was more at home, Henry James could be excellent company. I vividly recollect one Christmas dinner at the house of Sir Claude Phillips,[2] the art critic, when we all sat on the drawing-room floor and blew small feathers across a sheet. The face of Henry James, puffed with heroic effort, rising above the whiteness of the cloth, was irresistibly droll, though perfectly serious. Probably he played these childish games on Christmas night because he had a great liking for

* *As I Knew Them: Sketches of People I have Met on the Way* (London: Hutchinson, 1930) pp. 67–70.

Eugénie Phillips, Sir Claude's sister, whose friendship was of the rare and exquisite kind.

Henry James at home at Lamb House, Rye, was a much more genial person than the lion of London drawing-rooms. But he had, there, too, his odd unaccountable moments. He loved his beautifully proportioned Georgian house, with its large, white panelled rooms furnished in the 'period', and a butler who always reminded me of Cyrano de Bergerac.[3] How he could possibly have 'missed' the lovely amethyst-and-copper lustre tea service which I picked up one day, for ten shillings, almost within sight of his door I can only attribute to his habit of procrastination. His chagrin when I told him of my bargain was real. 'You don't mean to say – to say, my dear young lady – that you've actually bought it? For six weeks – for six weeks I have been deliberating – deliberating – whether I should acquire that tea-service – and now – in five minutes, yes, in five minutes, it is yours!' ...

That day he gave signs of the over-strain which he was suffering from when he was writing that *macabre* story, *The Turn of the Screw*. Having invited Mrs Hodgson Burnett[4] and the whole of her house-party to luncheon at Lamb House, he began the affair handsomely enough, talking to all his guests, playing the perfect host. Suddenly, in the middle, he got up from his place, walked out without any apology, and could be seen, by his amazed guests, pacing the green garden outside the windows in a brown study. Cyrano de Bergerac continued, meticulously, to hand the dishes, and no one said a word about the strange disappearance of our host. Neither did he make any pother about it when we met again, in the drawing-room, and he showed us, with all the householder's pride, the upstairs and downstairs of his engaging English home.

Henry James chose Rye as a residence because, he declared, he liked golfers in plus-fours. It was characteristic of him that he never wanted to talk 'literature', but was profoundly interested in Life. He himself has said that he was half an Englishman because, as a small boy ... he was always immersed in a newly arrived number of *Punch*.

The clip-clop of hansom cab horses on a wet and slightly foggy night in London would cause in Henry James the same kind of ecstasy as 'autumnal leaves which strew the brooks in Vallombrosa'[5] arouse in cultured English spinsters in quest of emotion on a first visit to Italy.

Another visit which I paid to Lamb House remains in my memory. A guest at Maytham Hall, Mrs Hodgson Burnett's country home, had acquired a motor-bicycle to which was attached a 'trailer', and on this truly infernal conveyance he persuaded me to go and see our mutual friend at Rye. The roads were then guileless of tar; the summer dust was thick and when we arrived, after much peril, at Lamb House, I was so white from head to foot that only with an effort could Henry James recognise this draggled creature out of a flour mill.

But our afternoon was a success. Our host was fresh from America (one of his rare visits) and he wanted to talk of his experiences. The bane of his visit, he said, had been 'the Japanese'. Students from that great country, of all shapes and sizes, speaking an incredible version of the English language, had pestered him all day and night. The rest of America, he declared, seemed to be inhabited by Italians, and you heard no English in the streets. As for New York, he said, it had been pulled down and rebuilt at least twice since his last visit; the city was, to the man who remembered it in the seventies and eighties, unrecognisable. To find an old friend in the same house was impossible.

Henry James's face was so tragic in repose, that when he smiled it was an event which made the whole room light up. Not long before he died, I was talking to Sir Claude Phillips in a picture gallery when we came across him face to face. The sad features lit up. 'And here is Claude', he murmured, 'and here is Ella . . .' as if he were counting over carefully the part (and mine was singularly insignificant) which we had, as individuals, played in his life. The little incident was as slight as one in a story of his own, but one could not forget it. If Henry James dwelt on trifles by the strange alchemy of his genius, they suddenly became of profound significance.

NOTES

1. Presumably an error for 'The Altar of the Dead', a story by James published in *Terminations* (1895).

2. Sir Claude Phillips (1846–1924), English art critic, became Keeper of the Wallace Collection.

3. Seventeenth-century French soldier and dramatist, the hero of a popular play (1898) by Edmond Rostand, where he is depicted as endowed with a nose of exceptional size. For another jesting reference to James's manservant Burgess, see p. 78.

4. Frances Hodgson Burnett (1849–1924), authoress, best known for *Little Lord Fauntleroy* and *The Secret Garden*.

5. *Paradise Lost*, I, lines 303–4.

'Carrying Lucidity to Dazzling Point'*

EDWARD MARSH

The first time I met Henry James was at one of Edmund Gosse's grander dinner-parties in Delamere Terrace. When the ladies went upstairs, I was left sitting next to him, and with inward tremors on my part a perfunctory conversation began. Gradually his eye lightened, and after a pause he went on in a warmer tone (what he says must be imagined with a punctuation of hesitant 'm–m's' and the accompaniment of a regular beat of his hand on the table, like a muffled minute drum). 'I wonder,' he said, 'if you would mind my asking what might seem, on so slight an acquaintance, m–m–a rather personal question.' I begged him to ask me anything he liked. 'How good of you! Then if you will forgive me for being so inquisitive, I *should* very much like to know–m–m–m–how long it is since you left Cambridge.' I thought this hardly warranted the compunction of his preamble, but I answered by the book–eighteen months, or whatever it was. 'Ah yes,' he said, 'just so, just so. But that wasn't–m–quite what I wanted to get – m – *at*. Upon my word, it seems an unpardonable intrusion, meeting you for the first time, to put such an intimate question – but – what I really want to know is – m – m – m – m – what is your age?' I told him the truth – twenty-four, I think it was; and he turned his full beam on me. 'Just so, just so,' he said again, 'but you look so delightfully young. But what an advantage that is, to combine the ... appearance of juvenility with the ... experience of maturity – in a word' (putting his hand on my shoulder, and in a tone of jubilance) 'the Flower of Youth with the Fruits of Time!'

Our second meeting was also at the Gosses', on the occasion of their annual New Year's Eve party. After seasonable refreshment downstairs, the guests would be led to a not very large room at the top of the house for some form of entertainment – usually quite a good one, but this time our

* *A Number of People* (London: Heinemann, 1939) pp. 114–18.

hosts had made an unlucky choice; and the literary lights of London, packed like figs in a box, observed with languor the performance of some third-rate marionettes. After a while Mr James, who was standing beside me, squeezed against a wall, turned to me with a malicious gleam in his eye. 'An interesting example, my dear Marsh, of Economy – Economy of Means – and – and – and –' (with an outburst) 'Economy of *Effect!*'

At about this time I told him I was going on a first visit to Paris, and he warned me against a possible disappointment in terms which were a choice example of what Mr Flosky in *Nightmare Abbey*[1] might have called his hyperoxysophistical paradoxology. 'Do not,' he said, 'allow yourself to be "put off" by the superficial and external aspect of Paris; or rather (for the *true* superficial and external aspect of Paris has a considerable fascination) by what I may call the superficial and external aspect *of* the superficial and external aspect of Paris.' This was surely carrying lucidity to dazzling point; I did my best to profit by it, but I couldn't be sure that I was exercising exactly the right discrimination, and in the end I surrendered to the charm of Paris without too much circumspection.

I never saw him at all regularly, but our occasional meetings were always a delight, even though his earnestness in matters of detail was sometimes an embarrassment. Once we left a dinner-party together, and after walking a little way hailed a hansom, in which I sat, while he stood for several minutes on the footboard discussing with the cabman the route which would best meet our dual needs. In vain I murmured from within: 'Oh, Mr James, do tell him the Reform Club, and I'll go on from there'; still he unrolled his mental map of London, hatching alternative itineraries. On another occasion we were walking and talking down Pall Mall, when for some special emphasis he turned half-left, pulling me round half-right to face him, and fixed me to the spot, with a hand on each shoulder, while we stood like a Siamese lighthouse amid the surge of pedestrians, and he tracked the *mot juste* through the maze of his large vocabulary.

Almost always I carried away something deliciously characteristic which has stuck in my memory ever since; some of my best treasures I cannot print, lest I wring withers; for though the kindliest of men, he never hid the workings of his critical sense, and I am writing on the principle ascribed to Crabbe by the authors of *Rejected Addresses*,[2] 'never to say anything which could give pain, however slight, to any individual, however wicked or foolish'. But here are one or two which I hope are anodyne.

Lady Arthur Russell,[3] while her husband was alive, had regularly given parties on Tuesday evenings at her house in Audley Square. Henry

James was one of the *habitués*, and he enjoyed going to see her on other days too, though he had been known to remark on the difficulty of making conversation 'under the eyes of that long row of silent, observant children'. When these same children grew up, the 'Tuesdays' were revived, partly for their friends, and partly for the survivors from the old days. I met him there on his first appearance, and he stood beside me, surveying the guests with 'no unpleasing melancholy'. 'It's a strange experience,' he said, 'to come back after all these years to the scene of so many memories – to find a few of the old familiar figures retired in the background, and the foreground filled with a mass of the portentous young, of whom, my dear Marsh' (and here came the beam of eye and voice) 'you are one.' I think it was to Lady Arthur, who had asked him if he knew the names of women's clothes, that he answered: 'I know a bertha – and a spencer – and a ruff.'

He gave me a depressing account of Holman Hunt's[4] conversation, which he likened to a trickle of tepid water from a tap one is unable to turn off. 'There must be some way,' he said, 'one could do *so*, or *so*, or *so*' (imitating the gesture of turning a tap this way and that), 'but no, nothing will stop it, on it goes. Once I had occasion to visit an obscure street in Chelsea, and after trying for some time to find it, in an evil hour' (here his voice became sinister) 'I met Holman Hunt, who professed knowledge of it and offered to guide me. And for two mortal hours we wandered through the byways of Chelsea, while he talked on and on and on. He chose the not unattractive subject of Ruskin's marriage; but even that topic, which might in other hands have been alluring, proved in his not otherwise than DULL.'

Two more tiny scraps: his reply, at a fabulous dinner of all the *sommités* in all the American worlds, given in his honour during his celebrated visit to New York, to a guest who gushed at him: 'Isn't this an interesting occasion, Mᵣ James?' 'Abysmally so, dear lady'; and his pensive answer to someone who asked what he supposed George Eliot's husband, J. W. Cross,[5] to have felt when she died: 'Regret . . . remorse . . . RELIEF.'

In later years we were brought closer together by our common friendship with Rupert Brooke,[6] for whom he had a strong admiration and affection. They met first at Cambridge, whither he had at long last been lured by repeated invitations from a small group of unknown admirers. He came back slightly disappointed in his hosts, but full of the young Apollo who had casually shone-in upon what he had evidently thought their rather dingy *milieu*. This was not long before Rupert's departure for America, and they cannot have seen much of each other; but I remember going with Rupert to luncheon with him in his Chelsea

flat and realising what a genuine relation had sprung up between the
older and the younger man.

NOTES

Sir Edward Howard Marsh (1872–1953), civil servant and author. In 1915 he
was attached to the Prime Minister's office, and on 18 December he wrote a long
memorandum to Asquith urging that the Order of Merit be conferred on James,
who was then seriously ill.

1. Peacock's novel was published in 1818.
2. Collection of parodies by James and Horace Smith, published in 1812.
3. Daughter of Earl Beauchamp and wife of Sir Arthur Russell, later Baron
Ampthill.
4. William Holman Hunt (1827–1910), English painter.
5. George Eliot married J. W. Cross in May 1880 and died in December of the
same year. Cross published a biography of George Eliot in 1885.
6. Rupert Brooke (1887–1915), poet. James met him on 13 June 1909 at
Pembroke College, Cambridge, at a lunch organised by Geoffrey Keynes (see
p. 45); later the young man is said to have punted James on the Cam. After
returning home James wrote in a letter that he had been made to 'loll not only
figuratively but literally on velvet surfaces exactly adapted to my figure', and
sent his thanks to all his Cambridge hosts 'with a definite stretch towards the
Rupert – with whose name I take this liberty because I don't know whether one
loves one's love with a (surname) terminal *e* or not'. When Brooke died of
blood-poisoning while on active service, James wrote: 'He was an interesting
young poet – he has left things, and they'll be gilded. But he was also such a
beautiful young being. *Youth*, however, was his sense, his scope, his limit – and
we shall think of him as of the family of Keats and Shelley.' James's last piece of
literary work was a preface for Brooke's posthumously published *Letters from
America* (1916).

'Great Individuality'*

ARNOLD BENNETT

I met Henry James twice. First in the office of Mr J. B. Pinker.[1] I was
amused in secret, because he was so exactly like the (quite good-

---

* *Things That Have Interested Me* (London: Chatto & Windus, 1921)
pp. 316–19.

humoured) caricatural imitations of him by H. G. Wells. But I was also deeply impressed, not to say intimidated. Although I was nearer fifty than forty I felt like a boy. He had great individuality. And there was his enormous artistic prestige, and his staggering technical skill in the manipulation of words. He asked me if I ever dictated. I said that I could dictate nothing but letters; that I had once dictated a chapter of a novel, but that the awful results decided me never to try it again. He said I might yet come to it. (I never shall.) He said he knew just how I felt, and that he had felt the same, but had got into the habit of dictation. (Certainly some of his dictated letters are complex masterpieces of dictation – unless he revised the copy afterwards.) He expressed stupefaction when I said that I knew nothing about the middle classes, and indicated that the next time he saw me he would have recovered from the stupefaction and the discussion might proceed. Talking about the material for novels, he maintained that there was too much to say about everything, and that was what was most felt by one such as himself, not entirely without – er – er – perceptions. When I told him that sometimes I lay awake at night, thinking of the things I had forgotten to put into my novels, he said that my novels were 'crammed', and that when something was 'crammed' nothing else could be put in, and so it was all right. He spoke with feeling about his recent illness: 'I have been very ill.'

At a later date, in the coffee room of the Reform Club he came up to me and said: 'You probably don't remember me. I'm Henry James.' I blushed. . . .

With all its faults my memory was incapable of forgetting a Henry James. He asked me if I was alone. I said I had two guests. He said: 'May I join your party upstairs?' I blushed again. It seemed to me incredible that Henry James should actually be asking to join my party. We received him with all the *empressement* that he desired. He talked. He did all the talking, and he was exceedingly interesting. He said that to him the Reform Club was full of ghosts. He told us about all the ghosts, one after another. There was no touch of sentimentality in his recollections. Everything was detached, just, passionless, and a little severe – as became his age. His ghosts were the ghosts of dead men, and his judgements on them were no longer at the mercy of his affections. He was not writing to them or to their friends. I doubt whether Henry James ever felt a passion, except for literature. I doubt whether he was, in life, more than a dilettante. And, if it was so, that is what is the matter with his novels. They lack ecstasy, guts.

NOTE

Arnold Bennett (1867–1931), highly successful novelist, dramatist and journalist, had been present at the first night of *Guy Domville*. On the occasion of the first meeting described he was already a well-established author, having published such works as *The Grand Babylon Hotel* (1902), *The Old Wives' Tale* (1908), *Clayhanger* (1910) and *Hilda Lessways* (1911). Bennett's letters contain many scattered references to James (*The Letters of Arnold Bennett*, ed. James Hepburn (London: Oxford University Press, 1966) 3 vols). Elsewhere in *Things That Have Interested Me*, a collection of reprinted essays and reviews, Bennett observes of James that 'his affections often overbore his unquestionable critical faculty' (p. 312). For James on Bennett, see pp. 23, 139.

1. Pinker was a well-known literary agent. The meeting referred to took place on 6 January 1913 and is described thus in Bennett's journal:

> *Henry James.* At Pinkers. Very slow talker. Beautiful French. Expressed stupefaction when I said I knew nothing about the middle-class, and said the next time he saw me he would have recovered from the stupefaction, and the discussion might proceed. Said there was too much to say about everything – and that was the first thing most felt by one such as he, not entirely without – er – er – er – er – perceptions. When I said I lay awake at nights sometimes thinking of the things I had left out of my novels, he said that all my stuff was crammed, and that when the stuff was crammed nothing more could be put in, and so it was all right. He spoke with feeling about his recent illness. 'I have been very ill.' Said he was now settled down in Cheyne Walk, and had one or two faithful dependable servants, and so on. An old man, waning, but with the persistent youthfulness that all old bachelors have. (*Journals*, ed. Newman Flower (London: Cassell, 1932–3) II, p. 57)

Part II

Places and People

James in Paris*

WILLIAM ROTHENSTEIN

Henry James often came to Paris, where he had numerous friends. He was *persona grata* among French writers, as well as among his own compatriots. He took a great fancy to Frazier, and often wandered into the studio in the rue Madame. He was charming to all of us; he liked young people, and all his life he had been closely associated with painters and sculptors. I was amused by his slow and exact way of speaking. He was not in those days so massive as he became later, either in person or manner, but he was already elaborately precise and correct. He always carried his silk hat, stick and gloves into the room when he paid a call, laying hat and gloves across his knee. I had not read his writings, and knew him only as a discerning lover of Paris, who delighted in its old streets and houses, and as an arresting talker, of course.

* *Men and Memories, 1872–1922* (London: Faber, 1931–2) I, p. 82.

NOTE

William Rothenstein (1872–1945), English painter, lived in Paris 1889–93.

James in Italy*

MRS HUMPHRY WARD

Our earliest guest was Henry James, and never did I see Henry James in a happier light. A new light too. For here, in this Italian country, and in

* *A Writer's Recollections* (London: Collins, 1918) pp. 325–9.

the Eternal City, the man whom I had so far mainly known as a Londoner was far more at home than I; and I realised perhaps more fully than ever before the extraordinary range of his knowledge and sympathies.

Roman history and antiquities, Italian art, Renaissance sculpture, the personalities and events of the Risorgimento, all these solid *connaissances* and many more were to be recognised perpetually as rich elements in the general wealth of Mr James's mind. That he had read immensely, observed immensely, talked immensely, became once more gradually and delightfully clear on this new field. That he spoke French to perfection was of course quickly evident to anyone who had even a slight acquaintance with him. M. Bourget[1] once gave me a wonderful illustration of it. He said that Mr James was staying with himself and Madame Bourget at their villa at Hyères, not long after the appearance of Kipling's *Seven Seas*. M. Bourget, who by that time read and spoke English fluently, complained of Mr Kipling's technicalities, and declared that he could not make head or tail of McAndrew's Hymn.[2] Whereupon Mr James took up the book, and standing by the fire, fronting his hosts, there and then put McAndrew's Hymn into vigorous idiomatic French – an extraordinary feat, as it seemed to M. Bourget. Something similar, it will be remembered, is told of Tennyson. 'One evening,' says F. T. Palgrave of the poet, 'he read out, off-hand, Pindar's great picture of the life of Heaven, in the Second Olympian, into pure modern prose splendidly lucid and musical.' Let who will decide which *tour de force* was the more difficult.

But Mr James was also very much at home in Italian, while in the literature, history and art of both countries he moved with the well-earned sureness of foot of the student. Yet how little one ever thought of him as a student! That was the spell. He wore his learning – and in certain directions he was learned – 'lightly, like a flower'. It was to him not a burden to be carried, not a possession to be proud of, but merely something that made life more thrilling, more full of emotions and sensations; emotions and sensations which he was always eager, without a touch of pedantry, to share with other people. His knowledge was conveyed by suggestion, by the adroitest of hints and indirect approaches. He was politely certain, to begin with, that you knew it all; then to walk *with you* round and round the subject, turning it inside out, playing with it, making mock of it, and catching it again with a sudden grip, or a momentary flash of eloquence, seemed to be for the moment his business in life. How the thing emerged, after a few minutes, from the long involved sentences! – only involved because the impressions of a man of genius are so many, and the resources of speech so limited. This involution, this deliberation in attack, this slowness of approach towards a point which in the end was generally triumphantly rushed, always seemed to me more effective as Mr James used it in speech than as he employed it – some of us would say, to excess – in a few of his latest books. For, in talk, his own living personality – his flashes of fun – of courtesy – of 'chaff' – were always there, to do away with what in the written word, became a difficult strain on attention.

I remember an amusing instance of it, when my daughter D[orothy], who was housekeeping for us at Castel Gandolfo, asked his opinion as to how to deal with the Neapolitan cook, who had been anything but satisfactory, in the case of a luncheon-party of friends from Rome. It was decided to write a letter to the ex-bandit in the kitchen, at the bottom of the fifty-two steps, requesting him to do his best, and pointing out recent short-comings. D——, whose Italian was then rudimentary, brought the letter to Mr James, and he walked up and down the vast *salone* of the villa, striking his forehead, correcting and improvising. 'A really nice pudding' was what we justly desired, since the Neapolitan genius for sweets is well known. Mr James threw out half phrases – pursued them – improved upon them – withdrew them – till finally he rushed upon the magnificent bathos – 'un dolce come si deve!'[3] – which has ever since been the word with us for the tip-top thing.

With the country people he was simplicity and friendship itself. I recollect him in close talk with a brown-frocked bare-footed monk, coming from the monastery of Palazzuola on the farther side of the Alban lake, and how the super-subtle, super-sensitive cosmopolitan found not the smallest difficulty in drawing out the peasant, and getting at something real and vital in the ruder, simpler mind. And again, on a never to be forgotten evening on the Nemi Lake, when on descending from Genzano to the strawberry farm that now holds the site of the famous temple of Diana Nemorensis, we found a beautiful youth at the *fattoria*, who for a few pence undertook to show us the fragments that remain. Mr James asked his name. 'Aristodemo',[4] said the boy, looking as he spoke the Greek name, 'like to a god in form and stature'. Mr James's face lit up; and he walked over the historic ground beside the lad, Aristodemo picking up for him fragments of terracotta from the furrows through which the plough had just passed, bits of the innumerable small *figurines* that used to crowd the temple walls as ex-votos, and are now mingled with the *fragole* in the rich alluvial earth. It was a wonderful evening; with a golden sun on the lake, on the wide stretches where the temple stood, and the niched wall where Lord Savile[5] dug for treasure and found it; on the great ship-timbers also, beside the lake, wreckage from Caligula's galleys, which still lie buried in the deepest depth of the water; on the rock of Nemi, and the fortress-like Orsini villa; on the Alban Mount itself, where it cut the clear sky. I presently came up with Mr James and Aristodemo, who led us on serenely, a young Hermes in the transfiguring light. One almost looked for the winged feet and helmet of the messenger god! Mr James paused – his eyes first on the boy, then on the surrounding scene. 'Aristodemo!' he murmured smiling, and more to himself than me, his voice caressing the word – 'what a name! what a place!'

NOTES

Mary Augusta Ward, neé Arnold (1851–1920), was a granddaughter of Dr Arnold of Rugby, a niece of Matthew Arnold, and the wife of Humphry Ward, leader-writer and art-critic for *The Times*. She was a prolific novelist and reviewer. (See biographies by Janet Penrose Trevelyan (1923) and Enid Huws Jones (1973).) James visited the Humphry Wards at their London home in Russell Square and in 1899 stayed with them at the Villa Barberini, a seventeenth-century Roman villa where Mrs Ward spent three months writing a novel about Italy. As Leon Edel has pointed out, she is in error in describing James as 'our earliest guest', for 'he was actually one of the last guests – he came at the end of her three months' stay' (*Treacherous Years*, p. 295). She later sent the proofs of *Eleanor*, the novel written during her time in Rome, to James, and he corresponded with her on the subject.

James published an article on Mrs Humphry Ward in the *English Illustrated Magazine* in February 1892, collected in *Essays in London and Elsewhere* (1893). For a reference to one of James's visits to the Humphry Wards' London home, see p. 72.

1. Paul Bourget (1852–1935), French novelist. He was introduced to James by Sargent in July 1884, and he and his wife became close friends of James and spent a good deal of time in his company during visits to England and Italy. James had a high regard for Bourget's conversational powers and described him as 'one of the most charming and ingenious talkers I ever met' and as 'an intellectual and colloquial luxury'.

2. Kipling's poem is dated 1893. Its language is rendered difficult by the use of Scots dialect and technical terms.

3. 'A pudding as it should be.'

4. The young man is mentioned in a letter written by James to Mrs Humphry Ward after her visit and also in her novel *Eleanor*.

5. In Oscar Wilde's *Lord Arthur Savile's Crime* (1891).

America Revisited*

ELIZABETH JORDAN

He found it greatly changed and was pained by many of the changes, which seemed to have borne out his worst forebodings. I was having some eye-trouble and eye-tests at this time, which meant that I was at home for a few days and moving in dimly lighted rooms. Mr James frequently dropped in to sit in this gloaming with me, and I shall always remember his understanding sympathy.

Incidentally, he poured forth his first vivid impressions of American life. He disliked America's noise, the sloppy speech of its people, their bad manners and frequent rudeness. As an instance of the rudeness he gave me a first-hand account of an experience with a young brakeman. The brakeman was passing through a railroad car in which Mr James was a passenger. The author stopped the lad and asked at what hour the train would reach a certain city. The brakeman looked at him, and passed on without replying.

'And that', Mr James sadly ended, 'was the end of an association which, although so brief, I had fondly hoped might be so pleasant.'

Most of all Mr James objected to what, in an impassioned moment, he called our 'damned orchids'. He seemed shocked by the oath even as it fell from his lips, but he made it clear that the 'damned orchids', which he seemed to be finding on every luncheon and dinner table where he sat as a guest, epitomised to him America's tendency toward vulgar ostentation.

In his turn he supplied Americans with a few disappointments. He remembered clearly and fondly the fine old literary guard of Boston and New York, but he had no knowledge of or interest in the literary newcomers. While he was here I gave a reception for him, to which I invited his available old friends, as well as our best group of up-and-coming young writers. The names of the latter meant nothing to him, and his hearty handclasps did not comfort them for the revelation

* *Three Rousing Cheers* (New York: Appleton, 1938) pp. 216–19.

conveyed by his vague smile. Some of the writers, both old and young, resented this. In presenting them to the Master I pronounced each name with almost piercing distinctness, but usually in vain. Hamlin Garland[1] was so affected by the unbroken calm with which his name was received that he broke out earnestly, 'I'm *Hamlin* Garland, Mr James!'

'A-h – h', said Mr James, and shook hands all over again, smiling cherubically. There is a story that when Miss Wilkins[2] was introduced to him very impressively as 'Miss Mary E. Wilkins, the *author*', Mr James brought out the smile again and said kindly, 'Ah, you *write*?'

I never believed that one.

My Gramercy Park apartment is diagonally across from the Players' Club. Mr James dropped in at tea-time one afternoon, as he had a pleasant way of doing, and told me the Players' Club was giving a stag dinner for him at eight o'clock that night.

'I know', I said. 'You're to make a speech, too. Mr Munro told me about it.'

Mr James immediately became very much agitated.

'But that's all a mistake', he cried passionately. 'I never made a speech in my life. I could not make a speech to *save* my life. I told the worthy Munro so. I made it clear to him. I thought he understood.'

'No, they're all expecting a speech', I said unfeelingly. 'They know you don't want to make a formal speech, but they're counting on you to stand up and chat with them as a friend and a brother.'

Mr James then looked so miserable that my heart ached for him.

'You have time to prepare a brilliant "extemporaneous" talk that will lift them out of their chairs', I reminded him.

Mr James stared thoughtfully into the fire.

'Ah – h – ' he murmured. 'A-h-h-h. Quite so.'

He swallowed a cup of tea and rushed away. David Munro, whose office was next to mine at Harper's, gave me the rest of the story the next morning. Mr James had made his 'extemporaneous' speech and had covered himself with glory. He had been wise and witty and altogether delightful.

'But the new experience and the applause and excitement went to his head', Mr Munro ended sadly. 'He kept getting up all evening to make more speeches.' . . .

I must also mention the deserved rebuke I overheard Mr James give a woman who was foolish enough to ask the Master the meaning of a certain passage in *The Wings of the Dove*.

'My dear lady,' Mr James said coldly, 'if after the infinite labour I give to my literature I am unable to convey to you my meaning, how can you expect me to do so by mere word of mouth?'

NOTES

Elizabeth Jordan was a young American journalist employed by the firm of Harper; she helped to organise James's public appearances during his visit to America in 1904–5.

1. See p. 94.
2. Mary E. Wilkins (1852–1930), prolific American author of short stories, novels and poems.

A Weekend in Cambridge*

GEOFFREY KEYNES

Friday, June 11th [1909], dawned at last and the triumvirate met Henry James at 6.19 p.m. at Cambridge station. James had written on June 5th to A. C. Benson: 'I go to Cambridge next Friday, for almost the first time in my life – to see a party of three friends whom I am in the singular position of never having seen in my life.' The meaning of 'almost' qualifying 'the first time' was at first obscure, since it was fully understood that this was the first time he had set foot in Cambridge. In fact he had paid one brief visit there in 1878 or 1879.[1] On the present occasion he was conveyed in a cab to 8 Trumpington Street, where dinner was served before going to a concert in the Guildhall. The music consisted of pieces by Parry, Stanford, Mendelssohn and Wagner, but it was not an exciting programme and James was frankly bored. Conversation continued afterwards at 8 Trumpington Street until midnight and was remembered afterwards as amusing and very pleasant. Among the subjects discussed was the poetry of Walt Whitman, James maintaining that it was impossible for any woman to write a good criticism of him or to get near his point of view. Had the concert been more enlivening it would have been a good beginning to the whole episode, but one unfortunate feature made itself felt almost from the first moment. Delight in James's style of conversation was always enhanced for his audience by his habit of ponderously groping for the right word at every turn of phrase with interminable mumblings and interjections. This worked so much on Sayle's kindly and helpful nature that he was unable to resist the impulse

* *Henry James in Cambridge* (Cambridge University Press, 1968) pp. 14–19.

to suggest the word that he felt sure must be the *mot juste*. Invariably the suggestion was wrong and the word was waved aside, but Sayle proceeded imperturbably to offer another suggestion at the next opportunity. The other members of the triumvirate were agonisingly aware of the mounting irritation suffered by their distinguished guest, but Sayle was unable to restrain himself, and it was afterwards felt that this was, perhaps, an important factor in forming James's decision to leave Cambridge a day sooner than he had originally intended.

In spite of this unfortunate lapse in tact by James's chief host, breakfast at 8 Trumpington Street on Saturday, June 12th, was a most pleasant meal. Later in the morning he was taken by Sayle to see King's Chapel and the University Library. Bartholomew was seen working in his compartment in the Library and James, looking at him through the glass partition, remarked: 'Il n'est pas gâté by this view.' At one o'clock an anxious undergraduate (for it was an unforgettable occasion in the life of so youthful a host as myself) was preparing to welcome him to luncheon in his rooms in Pembroke. The company invited was formed, rather oddly, of R. C. Punnett, Professor of Genetics, Sydney Cockerell, Director of the Fitzwilliam Museum, and Rupert Brooke.[2] There is no memory of the topics of conversation, but there is no doubt that James fell at once under the spell of Rupert Brooke. He was the only new acquaintance made by James during the Cambridge episode to become a friend thought worthy of several subsequent meetings in London.

After luncheon James was taken by Cockerell to the Fitzwilliam Museum, where he seemed much interested, and, over the displayed manuscripts, talked with great admiration of Byron and Tolstoy. At four o'clock there was a gathering in the lovely long Combination Room at St John's, J. W. Clark, Francis Cornford[3] and H. F. Stewart[4] being invited to meet James, and after tea there was a memorable perambulation through Queens' College to see the famous gallery in the President's Lodge and other charming rooms. A vivid memory remains of Henry James (a true American in his reactions to the splendours of a mediaeval University) pausing to look up at Erasmus's tower to exclaim, with hands raised in wonder, 'How intensely venerable!' The afternoon's sightseeing clearly gave James the greatest delight and there were no complaints (as he had indicated in his letter of May 20th that there would not be) at having missed a view of the May Races on the river. In the evening James dined with his triumvirate at the Union, and he was taken to see a play at the ADC Theatre. He had anticipated much enjoyment from this, as the play (*The Return of the Prodigal*) was by his friend St John Hankin,[5] but it was a long drawn-out disappointment, and the chief pleasure for his hosts was James's conversation during the intervals. I drew him on to the subject of H. G. Wells, for whom he still, at this date, had great admiration. He declared that *Kipps* was the best novel of the last forty years. He talked also about modern plays, summing them up with the opinion that most of them should be neither acted nor read.

Sunday, June 13th, was ushered in by breakfast with Maynard Keynes[6] in King's. It is quite certain that on this occasion Henry James did not enjoy himself. He was bewildered by the clever scintillating conversation that eddied round him (this was confirmed by Maynard Keynes himself), and told afterwards of the incomprehensible utterances made by the Laughing Philosopher, as he called Harry Norton, one of Maynard's circle, who habitually followed every remark he made with senseless laughter and giggles. Thirty years later, in a review[7] of Sir Edward Marsh's *A Number of People*, Desmond MacCarthy[8] pretended to recall his memories of this occasion. It is quite plain that they were almost wholly inventions since they do not at all agree with the facts; nevertheless they are amusing enough to bear repetition and no doubt record, in a fictional setting, MacCarthy's impressions of the episode. He was a late arrival at the breakfast party and as he entered the room saw 'Henry James still sitting at the table, with a cold poached egg in front of him bleeding to death upon a too large, too thick helping of bacon, and surrounded by a respectful circle of silent, smoking, observant undergraduates. I saw again his bright, hazel-grey, prominent eyes signalling distress to me in the doorway – a latecomer but an old acquaintance – and the flustered eagerness of his greetings. "Tell me," he said, as soon as we were outside, "tell me about these remarkable young men, from whom, for some years past I have received a most flattering annual invitation. The beauty of this gorgeous summer, the remembered beauty of this august place, and, to be frank, also a small domestic upheaval not unconnected with plumbing, has at last induced me, as you perceive, to respond. I naturally expected to provide the fox, *to be* the fox, if I may compare myself to so agile and wary an animal, but I never foresaw that I should have also to furnish the hounds, the horses, the drags, the dog-carts, the terriers – in short the whole paraphernalia of a meet!" ' MacCarthy then shews James asking 'Who was the long quiet youth with fair hair who sometimes smiled?' and being told it was Rupert Brooke – though in fact James had already met Brooke the previous day. When told by MacCarthy that he wrote poetry, which was no good, James is reported to have said, 'Well, I must say I am *relieved*, for with *that* appearance if he had also talent it would be too unfair.' MacCarthy says that later he asked Brooke what James talked about, and was told, 'He gave me advice; he told me not to be afraid of being happy.' There is so much fiction in the rest of the story that it is impossible not to be suspicious of the truth of the last sentence. It seems more probable that James gave this advice at a much later meeting – if, indeed, he ever gave it at all.

After this uncomfortable experience James returned to the less exacting company of his triumvirate, luncheon being at 8 Trumpington Street, with Desmond MacCarthy and Cosmo Gordon[9] of King's added to the group. The weather was perfect and the party sat after their meal in the little walled garden at the back of the apparently almost nonexistent house. James's conversation was brilliant, the best that his visit to Cambridge elicited, including a description of Carlyle lecturing and a vivid impression of Lady Ritchie, 'her style, all smiles and wavings of the pocket handkerchief'. James talked to MacCarthy and Sayle of J. K. Huysmans and Pierre Louÿs, dismissing them both with opprobrium. At 5.30 James and MacCarthy went to call on Sir George Darwin[10] at Newnham Grange. Sayle and Cosmo Gordon accompanied James to dinner with J. W. Clark,[11] where there was great talk about Racine, Molière, *Hernani* and *Marion de Lorme* (by Victor Hugo), accompanied by 1847 port. The party came back to another gathering in Sayle's garden for coffee, being joined there by Rupert Brooke, Stewart Wilson of King's and George Mallory[12] of Magdalene. James's talk included a discussion of dancing and he told us also of the frontispieces to be added to the new edition of his works.

Monday, June 14th, was another lovely day, and after breakfast one of us suggested taking our guest on the river in a punt. Accordingly, towards midday, his bulky form was disposed on the cushions of a punt, hatless and completely at ease. The process of pushing off from the landing stage was marred when Sayle dropped the pole with a crack on the large, shiny, yellowish dome of James's bald head. Fortunately no serious harm was done, and Rupert Brooke, who had joined Sayle and myself for this enterprise, then assumed the task of poling the punt. Henry James enjoyed the unaccustomed experience to the full and an unforgettable image of him remains, lying comfortably on the cushions and gazing up through prominent half-closed eyes at Brooke's handsome figure clad in white shirt and white flannel trousers (for shorts were not worn by undergraduates in those days). This floating idyll lasted for more than an hour, while little conversation was possible, and the party then went to luncheon in Bartholomew's rooms at Kellet Lodge, Tennis Court Road, being joined by Cosmo Gordon. After the meal a final gathering assembled in Sayle's garden for coffee, including Desmond MacCarthy and Francis Thompson of Pembroke.

James had made a rather suddent decision to leave that afternoon instead of next morning and he was seen off by the triumvirate in the 4.35 train, the cab in which he left 8 Trumpington Street seeming to be piled with an extraordinary number of hats considering the shortness of his visit. At the station James conducted a delicious and inimitable leave-taking, during which Sayle must surely have still been suggesting the suitable words, though no accurate memory of this remains.

So ended a memorable episode, which Percy Lubbock[13] has some-where stated that James summarised by saying that he had 'met hundreds and hundreds of undergraduates all exactly alike'. Sydney Cockerell also recalled that James wrote to someone that he had been entertained at Cambridge 'by young men whose mother's milk was barely dry on their lips'; he had probably expected to be entertained by more senior university types. Yet his three hosts had not gathered an impression that he was in any way discontented. In discussions after-wards the visit was decided to have been on the whole a success. Except for the King's breakfast party their guest had obviously enjoyed almost everything in varying degree, with the river voyage as a suitable climax to the succession of events.

NOTES

Sir Geoffrey Keynes (born 1887), surgeon and bibliographer, brother of John Maynard Keynes (1883–1946), the economist. James spent a long weekend in Cambridge in June 1909 as the guest of Geoffrey Keynes (then a medical student), Charles Sayle (Under-Librarian at the University Library) and Theodore Bartholomew (Assistant Librarian). Before the visit James wrote to a friend that he felt 'rather like an unnatural intellectual Pasha visiting his Circassian Hareem!' Afterwards he wrote that 'they were as kind to me as possible and I *liked* it, the whole queer little commerce, and *them*, the queer little all juvenile gaping group, quite sufficiently'. His verdict on Cambridge was that 'in detail, I think, it beats Oxford; though inferior in *ensemble*' (see *Master*, pp. 403–5).

Geoffrey Keynes's account was originally written for a BBC Third Program-me broadcast on 25 December 1958 – almost half a century after the visit. A version appeared in the *London Magazine* in March 1959, and it was revised and corrected for broadcasting and publication in 1967.

1. James had previously visited Cambridge in 1878 or 1879; that visit is described in an article published in *Lippincott's Magazine* in April 1879 ('English Vignettes') and reprinted in *Portraits of Places* (1883) and *English Hours* (1905).

2. See p. 34.

3. Francis Cornford (1874–1943), Fellow of Trinity, later became Professor of Ancient Philosophy at Cambridge.

4. Hugh Fraser Stewart (1863–1948), Fellow of Trinity, became University Librarian.

5. St John Hankin (1869–1909), journalist and dramatist.

6. See above.

7. Published in the *Sunday Times* on 26 March 1939.

8. See p. 132.

9. Sir Cosmo Edmund Duff Gordon (1862–1931).

10. Sir George Howard Darwin (1845–1912), Professor of Astronomy and Experimental Philosophy at Cambridge.

11. Probably John Willis Clark (1833–1910), Registrar of the University of Cambridge from 1891.

12. George Mallory (1886–1924) of Magdalene College. Later well-known as a mountaineer, he died in an attempt on the summit of Everest.

13. Percy Lubbock (1879–1965), author of *The Craft of Fiction* (1921).

James on Zola*

HENRY HYNDMAN

I was walking back with Henry James very late one night from Putney to Piccadilly more than thirty years ago: walking because we had missed the last train, there were no buses, and cabs and cabbies had betaken themselves to their rest. It was a fine night, and the long walk and conversation were to me very pleasant.

But Zola![1] I had said good words of Zola, and had declared that the novelist was a very great writer. Then it came. Henry James, who, truth to say, I had always looked upon as a man of a mild temperament, one not given to letting his parts of speech get the better of him under any provocation whatsoever, vouchsafed to me his ideas on Zola and that unholy Frenchman's degradation of literature, with a power of expression that left nothing to the imagination, in respect either of directness or force. He stood still in the middle of the road to do it: he could not spare breath for perambulation while the paroxysm lasted.

* *Further Reminiscences* (London: Macmillan, 1912) p. 484.

NOTE

Henry Mayers Hyndman (1842–1921), journalist and political agitator.
1. Emile Zola (1840–1902), French novelist. The publication of English translations of his novels made his name a byword for moral offensiveness; in 1888 the National Vigilance Association conducted a successful prosecution against the publisher Henry Vizetelly for issuing his books. James published an essay on Zola in the *Atlantic Monthly* in August 1903 and included it in *Notes on Novelists* (1914).

On Gissing and Meredith*

SYDNEY WATERLOW

... the quality of his integrity still shines for me, however dimly, from these notes of his talk made in 1907 and 1908:

'How surprising that with so much humming and hawing, such deliberation in the choice of the right adjective, the portraits of persons that he builds up in talk should be so solid and vivid! Thus he described the only occasion on which he had seen Gissing.[1] The impression made by Gissing was a peculiarly painful one. Nature had been unkind to him. The front face was not bad; he had a fine forehead and clustering hair. But when he turned his head you saw one side of the face disfigured by a great expanse of purple scar, and mouth and chin were uncomely and feeble. Altogether an extraordinarily ungainly, common, ill-shaped figure; almost knock-kneed, bearing the unmistakable stamp of Wakefield, his birthplace. And how queer that such a being should speak French so well – with a precise affectation that made it almost *too* well!'

'He spoke of George Meredith[2] in terms of generous admiration – of the heroism of his life, his struggle against poverty and adversity, the high and gallant spirit with which he sat and watched bodily decrepitude creep on, with never a syllable of complaint. But he had been rereading

* 'Memories of Henry James', *New Statesman*, XXVI (6 February 1926) pp. 514–15.

the Italian novels and was astonished to find in how many ways they managed to be incredibly bad, with such a vagueness of idea and plan that you never know where you are or what it is all about; and yet there are those scenes of exquisite beauty, with the breath of greatness blowing through it all. *Vittoria*[3] is like the opening of a series of windows on history; but only glimpses, things are never done from the inside. Henry James is beset by a sense of the immense difficulty of being really inside anything; thus the Italian events had been of his own time, and he feels it impossible that anyone should adequately reproduce their real proportions and complexities. Certain recent handlings of the Risorgimento in a spirit of artless Macaulay-cum-Arnold rigidity he dismissed with scorn; but how far from the realities is even a genius like George Meredith! Think, for instance, of his enthusiasm for French things and his fancied immersion in the French character; and all the time how profoundly, how extravagantly misinformed! And what are we to make of the England he draws? An England of fabulous 'great' people, of coaching, prize-fighting and yachting, flavoured with the regency, yet incapable of precise location in space and time.'

The victory of Henry James's art may not have been worth winning, but a victory it was, a harmonisation of incongruities. And I find in these fragments the essence of the discord he resolved: on the one hand the sense of difficulty and responsibility – the enormous difficulty of getting inside the skin of life's complexities, the responsibility for rejecting every easy external solution; on the other, the shrinking from the common and unclean, the clinging to the ordered safe surface of well-to-do existence. It would be wrong to take this shrinking and clinging as evidence of any mistake about the nature of ultimate values; rather it is the shifts to which a powerful spirit, concerned with nothing but ultimate values, is put by some inner need to transpose all values into a key which will seem trivial, nay comic, to all but the uninitiated. Only on such terms was self-expression possible for him at all. Not that he would not sometimes speak out, as my faded records show, though within narrow limits, and always with an aversion from the concrete fact.

'He talked of politics, the immense waste of talk and energy and solemnity that Parliament is. He often wondered how so complex and cumbrous a machine as the British Empire managed to go on at all; there must be some mysterious tough element in it; perhaps it was easier for it to go on than to stop. The older he grew the more acutely and passionately did he feel the huge absurdity and grotesqueness of things, the monstrous perversity of evil. His taste became more and more delicate and sensitive. On my wondering why anyone should attach

importance to *taste*, "Attach importance!" he burst out, "that isn't what
one ever does or did to it. Why, it attaches importance to me!" He felt
tempted to call himself a rabid Socialist, so often does a great wind carry
him off his feet and set him down somewhere far beyond and ahead of the
present world.'

NOTES

Sir Sydney Philip Waterlow (1878–1944), British diplomat (knighted 1935),
was a Rye neighbour of Henry James. While at Cambridge he had been a
member of a circle that included Lytton Strachey, J. M. Keynes and Virginia
Woolf. His diary, now in the Berg Collection at the New York Public Library,
contains numerous references to James. See Leon Edel, 'Henry James and Sir
Sydney Waterlow', *Times Literary Supplement* (August 1968) pp. 844–5.
 1. George Gissing (1857–1903), English novelist. H. G. Wells introduced
Gissing to James in June 1901; for an account of this meeting see *The Master*,
p. 97.
 2. George Meredith (1828–1909), English novelist and poet. For another
account of James's views on Meredith, see Edith Wharton, *A Backward Glance*,
pp. 230–3.
 3. Meredith's novel *Vittoria* was published in 1867. Its subject is the Italian
revolution of 1848.

James on Ellen Terry*

EDMUND GOSSE

I can cap your entertaining recollection by another, which I dared not
print: H.J. was complaining to us that Ellen Terry[1] had asked him to
write a play for her, and now that he had done so, and read it to her, had
refused it. My wife, desiring to placate, asked: 'Perhaps she did not think
the part suited to her?' H.J. turned upon us both, and with resonance
and uplifting voice replied: 'Think? *Think?* How should the poor,
toothless, chattering hag THINK?' The sudden outpouring of improvised

* *John Bailey, 1864–1931: Letters & Diaries* (London: John Murray, 1935)
pp. 203–4.

epithets had a most extraordinary effect. A crescendo on 'toothless' and then on 'chattering' and then on 'hag' – and 'think' delivered with the trumpet of an elephant.

NOTE

On Edmund Gosse, see p. 10. The extract is taken from a letter to John Bailey written on 14 April 1920, and the phrase 'which I dared not print' refers to Gosse's recollections of James published in the *London Mercury*.

    1. On Ellen Terry, see p. 22. The reference seems to be to James's one-act play *Summersoft*, sent to Ellen Terry in August 1895. She seems to have been pleased with the play, but never produced it; three years later James turned it into a short story under the title 'The Two Magics' (see *The Complete Plays of Henry James*, pp. 519–20).

James and Belloc: an Encounter*

G. K. CHESTERTON

One summer we took a house at Rye, that wonderful inland island, crowned with a town as with a citadel, like a hill in a medieval picture. It happened that the house next to us was the old oak-panelled mansion which had attracted, one might almost say across the Atlantic, the fine aquiline eye of Henry James. For Henry James, of course, was an American who had reacted against America; and steeped his sensitive psychology in everything that seemed most antiquatedly and aristocratically English. In his search for the finest shades among the shadows of the past, one might have guessed that he would pick out that town from all towns and that house from all houses. It had been the seat of a considerable patrician family of the neighbourhood, which had long ago decayed and disappeared. It had, I believe, rows of family portraits, which Henry James treated as reverently as family ghosts. I think in a

---

* *Autobiography* (London: Hutchinson, 1936) pp. 218–22.

way he really regarded himself as a sort of steward or custodian of the mysteries and secrets of a great house, where ghosts might have walked with all possible propriety. The legend says (I never learned for certain if it was true) that he had actually traced that dead family-tree until he found that there was far away in some manufacturing town, one unconscious descendant of the family, who was a cheerful and common-place commercial clerk. And it is said that Henry James would ask this youth down to his dark ancestral house, and receive him with funereal hospitality, and I am sure with comments of a quite excruciating tact and delicacy. Henry James always spoke with an air which I can only call gracefully groping; that is not so much groping in the dark in blindness as groping in the light in bewilderment, through seeing too many avenues and obstacles. I would not compare it, in the unkind phrase of Mr H. G. Wells, to an elephant trying to pick up a pea. But I agree that it was like something with a very sensitive and flexible proboscis, feeling its way through a forest of facts; to us often invisible facts. It is said, I say, that these thin straws of sympathy and subtlety were duly split for the benefit of the astonished commercial gentleman, while Henry James, with his bowed dome-like head, drooped with unfathomable apologies and rendered a sort of silent account of his stewardship. It is also said that the commercial gentleman thought the visit a great bore and the ancestral home a hell of a place; and probably fidgeted about with a longing to go out for a B and S and the *Pink 'Un*.[1]

Whether this tale be true or not, it is certain that Henry James inhabited the house with all the gravity and loyalty of the family ghosts; not without something of the oppressive delicacy of a highly cultured family butler. He was in point of fact a very stately and courteous old gentleman; and, in some social aspects especially, rather uniquely gracious. He proved in one point that there was a truth in his cult of tact. He was serious with children. I saw a little boy gravely present him with a crushed and dirty dandelion. He bowed; but he did not smile. That restraint was a better proof of the understanding of children than the writing of *What Maisie Knew*. But in all relations of life he erred, if he erred, on the side of solemnity and slowness; and it was this, I suppose, that got at last upon the too lively nerves of Mr Wells; who used, even in those days, to make irreverent darts and dashes through the sombre house and the sacred garden and drop notes to me over the garden wall. I shall have more to say of Mr H. G. Wells and his notes later; here we are halted at the moment when Mr Henry James heard of our arrival in Rye and proceeded (after exactly the correct interval) to pay his call in state.

Needless to say, it was a very stately call of state; and James seemed to fill worthily the formal frock-coat of those far-off days. As no man is so dreadfully well-dressed as a well-dressed American, so no man is so terribly well-mannered as a well-mannered American. He brought his brother William with him, the famous American philosopher; and though William James was breezier than his brother when you knew him, there was something finally ceremonial about this idea of the whole family on the march. We talked about the best literature of the day; James a little tactfully, myself a little nervously. I found he was more strict than I had imagined about the rules of artistic arrangement; he deplored rather than depreciated Bernard Shaw, because plays like *Getting Married*[2] were practically formless. He said something complimentary about something of mine; but represented himself as respectfully wondering how I wrote all I did. I suspected him of meaning why rather than how. We then proceeded to consider gravely the work of Hugh Walpole, with many delicate degrees of appreciation and doubt; when I heard from the front-garden a loud bellowing noise resembling that of an impatient fog-horn. I knew, however, that it was not a fog-horn; because it was roaring out, 'Gilbert! Gilbert!' and was like only one voice in the world; as rousing as that recalled in one of its former phrases, of those who

> Heard Ney shouting to the guns to unlimber
> And hold the Beresina Bridge at night.

I knew it was Belloc,[3] probably shouting for bacon and beer; but even I had no notion of the form or guise under which he would present himself.

I had every reason to believe that he was a hundred miles away in France. And so, apparently, he had been; walking with a friend of his in the Foreign Office, a co-religionist of one of the old Catholic families; and by some miscalculation they had found themselves in the middle of their travels entirely without money. . . .

They started to get home practically without money. Their clothes collapsed and they managed to get into some workmen's slops. They had no razors and could not afford a shave. They must have saved their last penny to recross the sea; and then they started walking from Dover to Rye; where they knew their nearest friend for the moment resided. They arrived, roaring for food and drink and derisively accusing each other of having secretly washed, in violation of an implied contract between tramps. In this fashion they burst in upon the balanced tea-cup and tentative sentence of Mr Henry James.

Henry James had a name for being subtle; but I think that situation was too subtle for him. I doubt to this day whether he, of all men, did not miss the irony of the best comedy in which he ever played a part. He left America because he loved Europe, and all that was meant by England or France; the gentry, the gallantry, the traditions of lineage and locality, the life that had been lived beneath old portraits in oak-panelled rooms. And there, on the other side of the tea-table, was Europe, was the old thing that made France and England, the posterity of the English squires and the French soldiers; ragged, unshaven, shouting for beer, shameless above all shades of poverty and wealth; sprawling, indifferent, secure. And what looked across at it was still the Puritan refinement of Boston; and the space it looked across was wider than the Atlantic.

NOTES

Gilbert Keith Chesterton (1874–1936), essayist, novelist, critic and poet. The episode in question seems to belong to the summer of 1908. On 27 July 1908, Theodora Bosanquet, James's secretary, noted in her diary: 'In the course of the morning Mr James made me go and peep through the curtain to see "the unspeakable Chesterton" pass by – a sort of elephant with a crimson face and oily curls. He [James] thinks it very tragic that his mind should be imprisoned in such a body' (quoted in *Master*, p. 373).

1. A brandy and soda and a sporting newspaper.
2. Produced at the Haymarket Theatre in 1908.
3. Hilaire Belloc (1870–1953), novelist, poet and prolific author of essays, biography, travel books and historical studies. His *The Path to Rome* (1902) describes a walking tour through France and Switzerland to Italy.

James on Max Beerbohm*

EDMUND GOSSE

Henry James has been eating his Christmas dinner here with us, and I am anxious to let you know that he started the subject of your *Christmas Garland*,[1] and discussed it with the most extraordinary vivacity and

---

* Evan Charteris, *The Life and Letters of Sir Edmund Gosse* (London: Heinemann, 1931) pp. 350–1.

appreciation. He was full of admiration. I told him that you had a certain
nervousness about his acceptance of your parody of him, and he desired
me to let you know at once that no one can have read it with more wonder
and delight than he. He expressed himself in superlatives. He called the
book 'the most intelligent that has been produced in England for many a
long day'. But he says you have destroyed the trade of writing. No one,
now, can write without incurring the reproach of somewhat ineffectively
imitating – *you!* What could be more handsome? And alas! my dear Max,
what can be more true?

NOTE

On Edmund Gosse, see p. 10. The extract is taken from a letter written from
Gosse's London home (17 Hanover Terrace) on Christmas night, 1913. For Max
Beerbohm's account of James and a note on Beerbohm, see p. 139.
   1. Beerbohm's volume of parodies *A Christmas Garland* (1912) includes 'The
Mote in the Middle Distance', a brilliant parody of James's later prose style. In
his diary for February 1913, Sydney Waterlow describes a walk with James in
which the latter commented on the parody. He expressed himself as 'delighted
with Max's parody of himself, only it affected him in a curious way; whatever he
wrote now, he felt that he was parodying himself. He said the book was a little
masterpiece, but deplored the cruelty of some of the attacks.' James added that
there was to his mind 'something unpleasant about a talent which turned
altogether to exposing the weaknesses of others. It was indelicate' (quoted in
Master, p. 395). On a later parody by Beerbohm – happily never read by James –
see p. 155.

Part III

Occasions

The American is Staged*

ALICE JAMES

The great family event, over which I have been palpitating for the last 18 months or more has come off: *The American*[1] was acted for the first time at Southport, which they call the Brighton of Liverpool, on January 3rd, and seems to have been, as far as audience, Compton and author were concerned, a brilliant success. H. says that Compton acted admirably, and it was delightful to hear and see him (Harry) flushed with the triumph of his first ovation. At the end, he was called for with great insistence, and pushed onto the stage by the delighted and sympathetic company; at the third bow and round of applause, Compton, who was standing with him, turned and seized both his hands and wrung them; very pretty of him, wasn't it? I am so thankful that the dear being has had such a success. The 'first nights' to come, we shall be less quivering about. The Comptons, who are the best judges of the pulse of an audience, are radiant about the prospects of the play.

H. says that at about four o'clock he got so nervous that his knees began almost to knock together, that he couldn't eat any dinner, and went off to the theatre and walked about the stage, dusted the mantel-piece, set the pasteboard vases straight, turned down the corners of the rugs, after his usual manner in my apartments, when lo! as soon as the curtain went up, he became as calm as a clock. If H. should have dramatic success now, it will be a very interesting illustration of the law that you cannot either escape or hasten the moment. Almost two years ago he got a letter from Compton, asking him to dramatise *The American* for him; he was going to answer 'no', immediately, when he said to himself 'No, I'll think about it for a week', and the result has been this beautiful play, for beautiful it is, with its strongly human quality.

As self-revelations are the supreme interest, the following anecdote in its rounded completeness is valuable, apart from its comicality. William Archer,[2] the dramatic critic of the *World* who, Harry says, is far and

* *The Diary of Alice James*, pp. 161–2, 163.

away the best of his kind in London, wrote to Harry proposing to go to see the play at Southport. H. discouraged his doing so, on the grounds of the distance and the cold, but he was there, notwithstanding, on Saturday night; and Harry, who had never met him before, was introduced to him in one of the entreactes. After the play was over, he told Balestier[3] to tell Harry that he wished to speak to him at the hotel. On returning, H. sent a message inviting him to his sitting-room: upon his entrance, Archer murmured some words of congratulation upon H's success, adding immediately, 'I think it's a play that would be much more likely to have success in the Provinces than in London', and then he began, as by divine mission, to enumerate all its defects and flaws, and asked why H. had done so-and-so, instead of just the opposite, etc., etc. To H., of course, heated from his triumph, these uncalled-for and depressing amenities from an entire stranger seemed highly grotesque, none the less so, that to the eye, by his personal type (that of a dissenting minister), the young man seemed by nature, divorced from all matters theatrical. In spite of the gloom cast over his spirits, H. was able to receive it all with perfect urbanity, and the Comptons etc. coming in to supper before long, he bowed him out, and served him up as a delectable dish of roast prig, done to a turn. . . .

When you come upon these forms of existence, absolutely destitute of imagination and humour, can you wonder at the maddening irritation with which the critic fills the artist soul? who whatever he may not have done has at least *attempted* to create. H. replies, 'No, but one is so inadequate for it, and would have to be a Frenchman to hate them enough, and to express the irony, scorn and contempt with which one ought to be filled!' H., with his impervious mildness, certainly *is* inadequate to the subject, and remains completely unruffled by the whole fraternity. Apropos of literary inclination, Lady Lonsdale,[4] now Lady something else, asked Harry to come to see her at a certain hour one day, as she had something of great importance to consult him about; when H. arrived, she told him that she wanted to write a book about Boucher and Watteau and she wanted him to tell her how to begin a book, to which H. replied 'that there is no difficulty in beginning, the trouble is to leave off'.

NOTES

On Alice James, see p. 3. This diary entry is dated 7 January 1891.

1. A dramatisation of James's novel *The American* was produced at the Winter Garden Theatre, Southport, Lancashire, on 3 January 1891; a provincial tour

followed, and on 26 September it opened in London. On 30 December 1891 Alice James wrote in her diary: '*The American* died an honourable death, on the 76th night. It seemed, as far as the interest and enthusiasm of the audience went, a great success, but owing to a disastrous season for all the theatres, and Compton being new and impecunious, the run was shorter than we hoped' (p. 224). Edward Compton, the producer, was an actor and father of Compton Mackenzie (see p. 12).

2. William Archer (1856–1924), prominent drama critic, playwright and translator of Ibsen.

3. Charles Wolcott Balestier (1861–1891), writer and publisher. James wrote a preface for his posthumously published volume *The Average Woman* (1892).

4. Lady Lonsdale, formerly Lady Constance Herbert, was a sister of the Earl of Pembroke and the widow of the Earl of Lonsdale.

The First Night of *Guy Domville**

H. G. WELLS

[On 3 January 1895 Wells attended a performance of Oscar Wilde's play *An Ideal Husband,* and reviewed it for the *Pall Mall Gazette.*] On the fifth I had to do *Guy Domville,* a play by Henry James at the St James's Theatre. This was a more memorable experience. It was an extremely weak drama. James was a strange unnatural human being, a sensitive man lost in an immensely abundant brain, which had had neither a scientific nor a philosophical training, but which was by education and natural aptitude alike, formal, formally aesthetic, conscientiously fastidious and delicate. Wrapped about in elaborations of gesture and speech, James regarded his fellow creatures with a face of distress and a remote effort at intercourse, like some victim of enchantment placed in the centre of an immense bladder. His life was unbelievably correct and his home at Rye one of the most perfect pieces of suitably furnished Georgian architecture imaginable. He was an unspotted bachelor. He had always been well off and devoted to artistic ambitions; he had experienced no tragedy and he

* *Experiment in Autobiography: Discoveries and Conclusions of a Very Ordinary Brain (since 1866)* (London: Gollancz, 1934) II, pp. 535–8.

shunned the hoarse laughter of comedy; and yet he was consumed by a gnawing hunger for dramatic success. In this performance he had his first and last actual encounter with the theatre.

Guy Domville was one of those rare ripe exquisite Catholic Englishmen of ancient family conceivable only by an American mind, who gave up the woman he loved to an altogether coarser cousin, because his religious vocation was stronger than his passion. I forget the details of the action. There was a drinking scene in which Guy and the cousin, for some obscure purpose of discovery, pretended to drink and, instead, poured their wine furtively into a convenient bowl of flowers upon the table between them. Guy was played by George Alexander,[1] at first in a mood of refined solemnity and then as the intimations of gathering disapproval from pit and gallery increased, with stiffening desperation. Alexander at the close had an incredibly awkward exit. He had to stand at a door in the middle of the stage, say slowly 'Be keynd to Her. . . . *Be* keynd to Her' and depart. By nature Alexander had a long face, but at that moment with audible defeat before him, he seemed the longest and dismallest face, all face, that I have ever seen. The slowly closing door reduced him to a strip, to a line, of perpendicular gloom. The uproar burst like a thunderstorm as the door closed and the stalls responded with feeble applause. Then the tumult was mysteriously allayed. There were some minutes of uneasy apprehension. 'Author' cried voices. 'Au-thor!' The stalls, not understanding, redoubled their clapping.

Disaster was too much for Alexander that night. A spasm of hate for the writer of those fatal lines must surely have seized him. With incredible cruelty he led the doomed James, still not understanding clearly how things were with him, to the middle of the stage, and there the pit and gallery had him. James bowed; he knew it was the proper thing to bow. Perhaps he had selected a few words to say, but if so they went unsaid. I have never heard any sound more devastating than the crescendo of booing that ensued. The gentle applause of the stalls was altogether overwhelmed. For a moment or so James faced the storm, his round face white, his mouth opening and shutting and then Alexander, I hope in a contrite mood, snatched him back into the wings.

That was my first sight of Henry James with whom I was later to have a sincere yet troubled friendship. We were by nature and training profoundly unsympathetic. He was the most consciously and elaborately artistic and refined human being I ever encountered, and I swam in the common thought and feeling of my period, with an irregular abundance of rude knowledge, aggressive judgements and a disposition to get to close quarters with Madame Fact even if it meant a scuffle with her.

James never scuffled with Fact; he treated her as a perfect and unchallengable lady; he never questioned a single stitch or flounce of the conventions and interpretations in which she presented herself. He thought that for every social occasion a correct costume could be prescribed and a correct behaviour defined. On the table (an excellent piece) in his hall at Rye lay a number of caps and hats, each with its appropriate gloves and sticks, a tweed cap and a stout stick for the Marsh, a soft comfortable deerstalker if he were to turn aside to the Golf Club, a light-brown felt hat and a cane for a morning walk down to the Harbour, a grey felt with a black band and a gold-headed cane of greater importance, if afternoon calling in the town was afoot. He retired at set times to a charming room in his beautiful walled garden and there he worked, dictating with a slow but not unhappy circumspection, the novels that were to establish his position in the world of discriminating readers. They are novels from which all the fiercer experiences are excluded; even their passions are so polite that one feels that they were gratified, even at their utmost intimacy, by a few seemly gestures; and yet the stories are woven with a peculiar humorous, faintly fussy, delicacy, that gives them a flavour like nothing else in the language. When you want to read and find reality too real, and hard storytelling tiresome, you may find Henry James good company. For generations to come a select type of reader will brighten appreciatively to the *Spoils of Poynton, The Ambassadors, The Tragic Muse, The Golden Bowl* and many of the stories.

I once saw James quarrelling with his brother William James, the psychologist. He had lost his calm; he was terribly unnerved. He appealed to me, to me of all people, to adjudicate on what was and what was not permissible behaviour in England. William was arguing about it in an indisputably American accent, with an indecently naked reasonableness. I had come to Rye with a car to fetch William James and his daughter to my home at Sandgate. William had none of Henry's passionate regard for the polish upon the surfaces of life and he was immensely excited by the fact that in the little Rye inn, which had its garden just over the high brick wall of the garden of Lamb House, G. K. Chesterton was staying. William James had corresponded with our vast contemporary and he sorely wanted to see him. So with a scandalous directness he had put the gardener's ladder against that ripe red wall and clambered up and peeped over!

Henry had caught him at it.

It was the sort of thing that isn't done. It was most emphatically the sort of thing that isn't done.... Henry had instructed the gardener to put away that ladder and William was looking thoroughly naughty about it.

To Henry's manifest relief, I carried William off and in the road just outside the town we ran against the Chestertons who had been for a drive in Romney Marsh; Chesterton was heated and I think rather swollen by the sunshine; he seemed to overhang his one-horse fly; he descended slowly but firmly; he was moist and steamy but cordial; we chatted in the road for a time and William got his coveted impression.

NOTE

Herbert George Wells (1866–1946), novelist. At the beginning of 1895, he was appointed dramatic critic to the *Pall Mall*, a London daily. *Guy Domville* was his second assignment, and among other dramatic critics in the first-night audience were G. B. Shaw, Arnold Bennett and William Archer. James had written *Guy Domville* in the summer of 1893. It ran in London for only four weeks, and was succeeded by Wilde's *The Importance of Being Earnest*. For contemporary criticisms of the play by Shaw and others, see *The Complete Plays of Henry James*, pp. 479–82. On Wells's subsequent friendship and eventual quarrel with James, see *Henry James and H. G. Wells: A Record of their Friendship, their Debate on the Art of Fiction, and their Quarrel*, ed. Leon Edel and Gordon N. Ray (London: Hart-Davis, 1958).

1. George Alexander (1858–1918), actor–manager and matinée idol, was manager and lessee of the St James's Theatre. James wrote *Guy Domville* for him, and Alexander appeared in the title role.

'An Exhibition of Brutality'*

F. ANSTEY

Henry James, when I first knew him, wore a neat brown beard and had a striking resemblance to King Edward VII when Prince of Wales. In later years he was clean-shaven, which completely transformed him into the likeness of a particularly subtle abbé.

In conversation he was meticulously (no other adverb is so appropriate) careful to convey his precise meaning, so that his remarks became a sort of Chinese nest of parentheses; it took him some time to arrive at

* *A Long Retrospect* (Oxford University Press, 1936) pp. 140–3.

his point but he always reached it, and it was always well worth waiting for.

On occasions, however, he would be not only accurate but concise. I met him at a dinner-party once, shortly before the production of a play of his, and his hostess asked him if he did not find rehearsals a great strain. To which he replied: 'I have been sipping the – er – cup of Detachment.' No phrase could be a more perfect description of the state of mind to which most dramatists find themselves reduced at a certain stage of rehearsals. . . .

Henry James never wrote a play that had any great success on the stage; he had great gifts, but the sense of the theatre was not one of them. The minute analysis of impressions and motives which distinguishes his novels could hardly be conveyed in dialogue, and though he condensed his dialogue to a form which he probably considered an inartistic compromise, it always remained more literary than dramatic.

'Every dramatist, my dear Guthrie,' I remember his saying to me, 'and by "dramatist" I mean a writer who seriously attempts that most difficult and elusive art of expressing his impressions of life in a dramatic form – be that form Tragedy, Comedy, Melodrama, or what you will – every dramatist, then, as he sits at his desk to evolve his conceptions, must first visualise, or have before his mental eye, the proscenium of a theatre. And above that proscenium an immense clock, its hands indicating the hour of eight-thirty. Those hands will move inexorably on, till they reach eleven, and that deplorably insufficient space of time is all that is allowed him in which to make the actions and motives, however intricate, of his dramatis personae intelligible to an audience which he dare not count upon as possessing more than the average degree of intelligence. In that busy period of two hours and a half – and even there I am considerably overstating it in omitting to deduct the time occupied by the two intervals, which may represent anything from twenty to thirty minutes – within two hours, then, he must present and solve the problem he has set himself, or he is doomed.'

When *The Man from Blankley's*[1] was in rehearsal, he asked me to tell him what the play was about; I did, and his comment was: 'A most interesting problem', which I'm afraid was not at all the light in which I had regarded it myself, though I suppose there is a sense in which any play may be considered as a problem to be worked out to a satisfactory solution. It was certainly Henry James's view.

I was one of the audience at the first night of his *Guy Domville* at the St James's – a very terrible first night indeed. It was a costume play; the period early Georgian; George Alexander[2] played the name-part and was extremely well supported, while the stage sets designed by Edwin Abbey were charming. For a time all seemed to be going well, the dialogue, being Henry James's, was exquisitely phrased, and the house listened to it attentively. But before the first act was over it was clear that the play was not gripping the audience; the coughs which are so infallible a sign of it grew more and more frequent. However, the house was full of his friends and admirers, and the applause at the end of the act was loud enough, though it came chiefly from the stalls and dress circle.

The second act went fairly well, until the entrance of one of the female characters in an extraordinary headdress like a gigantic fur muff. It had, I believe, been copied from a contemporary print, and was strictly of the period, but unfortunately it gave the gallery the excuse they had been waiting for, and from that moment the fate of the play was sealed. At the second curtain the applause from the lower parts of the house irritated the gallery into counter-demonstrations, and throughout the third act they constantly interrupted the performers by laughter and jeers. George Alexander, though quite unused to such a reception, kept his nerve admirably, and so did his company, but when the final curtain fell there was an exhibition of brutality by some of the audience which I have never before or since seen equalled in any theatre. Loud calls for 'Author' came from every part of the house, and when Henry James appeared, evidently hoping that by some miracle the play was saved, the applause was drowned by merciless booing and hissing from the gallery, which had a visibly withering effect on him.

The rest of us did our best, but no amount of clapping could prevail over those venomous boos, and Henry James retired, deadly pale but dignified, fully aware that his play had failed.

NOTES

F. Anstey, pseudonym of Thomas Anstey Guthrie (1856–1934), prolific author of light fiction best remembered for *Vice Versa* (1882) and *The Brass Bottle* (1900).

1. *The Man from Blankley's* was a volume of sketches by Anstey published in 1893. The title-piece had originally been contributed to *Punch* and was evidently dramatised.

2. See p. 66.

Guy Domville: the Aftermath*

EDMUND GOSSE

Henry James was positively storm-ridden with emotion before the fatal night, and full of fantastic plans. I recall that one was that he should hide in the bar of a little public-house down an alley close to the theatre, whither I should slip forth at the end of the second act and report 'how it was going'. This was not carried out, and fortunately Henry James resisted the temptation of being present in the theatre during the performance. All seemed to be going fairly well until the close, when Henry James appeared and was called before the curtain only to be subjected – to our unspeakable horror and shame – to a storm of hoots and jeers and catcalls from the gallery, answered by loud and sustained applause from the stalls, the whole producing an effect of hell broke loose, in the midst of which the author, as white as chalk, bowed and spread forth deprecating hands and finally vanished. It was said at the time, and confirmed later, that this horrible performance was not intended to humiliate Henry James, but was the result of a cabal against George Alexander.

Early next morning I called at 34 De Vere Gardens, hardly daring to press the bell for fear of the worst of news, so shattered with excitement had the playwright been on the previous evening. I was astonished to find him perfectly calm; he had slept well and was breakfasting with appetite. The theatrical bubble in which he had lived a tormented existence for five years was wholly and finally broken, and he returned, even in that earliest conversation, to the discussion of the work which he had so long and so sadly neglected, the art of direct prose narrative. And now a remarkable thing happened. The discipline of toiling for the caprices of the theatre had amounted, for so redundant an imaginative writer, to the putting on of a mental strait-jacket. He saw now that he need stoop no longer to what he called 'a meek and lowly review of the right ways to keep on the right side of a body of people who have paid

* 'Henry James', *London Mercury*, I (1920) p. 684; II (1920) p. 29.

money to be amused at a particular hour and place'. Henry James was
not released from this system of vigorous renunciation without a very
singular result. To write for the theatre the qualities of brevity and
directness, of an elaborate plainness, had been perceived by him to be
absolutely necessary, and he had tried to cultivate them with dogged
patience for five years. But when he broke with the theatre, the rebound
was excessive. I recall his saying to me, after the fiasco of *Guy Domville*,
'At all events, I have escaped for ever from the foul fiend Excision!' He
vibrated with the sense of liberation, and he began to enjoy, physically
and intellectually, a freedom which had hitherto been foreign to his
nature.

The abrupt change in Henry James's outlook on life, which was the
result of his violent disillusion with regard to theatrical hopes and
ambitions, took the form of a distaste for London and a determination,
vague enough at first, to breathe for the future in a home of his own by the
sea. He thought of Bournemouth, more definitely of Torquay, but finally
his fate was sealed by his being offered, for the early summer months of
1896, a small house on the cliff at Point Hill, Playden, whence he could
look down, as from an 'eagle's nest', on the exquisite little red-roofed
town of Rye and over the wide floor of the marsh of Sussex. When the
time came for his being turned out of this retreat, he positively could not
face the problem of returning to the breathless heat of London in August,
and he secured the Vicarage in the heart of Rye itself for two months
more. Here, as earlier at Point Hill, I was his guest, and it was wonderful
to observe how his whole moral and intellectual nature seemed to
burgeon and expand in the new and delicious liberty of country life. We
were incessantly in the open air, on the terrace (for the Vicarage, though
musty and dim, possessed, like the fresher Point Hill, a sea-looking
terrace), sauntering round the little town, or roving for miles and miles
over the illimitable flats, to Winchelsea, to Lydd, to the recesses of
Walland Marsh – even, on one peerless occasion, so far afield as to
Midley Chapel and the Romneys.
  Never had I known Henry James so radiant, so cheerful or so
self-assured. During the earlier London years there had hung over him a
sort of canopy, a mixture of reserve and deprecation, faintly darkening
the fullness of communion with his character; there always had seemed
to be something indefinably non-conductive between him and those in
whom he had most confidence. While the play-writing fit was on him this
had deepened almost into fretfulness; the complete freedom of intercourse which is the charm of friendship had been made more and more

difficult by an excess of sensibility. Henry James had become almost what the French call a *buisson d'épines*. It was therefore surprising and highly delightful to find that this cloud had ceased to brood over him and had floated away, leaving behind it a laughing azure in which quite a new and charming Henry James stood revealed. The summer of 1896, when by a succession of happy chances I was much alone with him at Rye, rests in my recollection as made exquisite by his serene and even playful uniformity of temper, by the removal of everything which had made intercourse occasionally difficult, and by the addition of forms of amenity that had scarcely been foreshadowed.

NOTE

On Gosse, see p. 10.

A Visit to Miss Pater*

RICHARD JENNINGS

[The habit of hesitation] came increasingly to mark his conversation, which exemplified his guiding rule that 'From the moment it is a question of projecting a picture, no particle that counts for memory or is appreciable to the spirit *can* be too tiny.' His discriminations delayed his argument and were disconcerting when rather loudly pronounced in hearing of those whose characters he sought to define. I once asked him to pay a call on the sole surviving sister of Walter Pater.[1] The poor lady lived much alone. I fear that the visit was not a success. Henry James was in a mood for the pursuit of tiny particles. Hester Pater glared at him and told him that she hated 'horrid' ghost stories about children. This turn of the screw became so painful that we soon rose to go. On the doorstep of the tiny house, whence he was perfectly audible from within, James discriminated long and loud in this manner:

* 'Fair Comment', *Nineteenth Century*, CXXXIII (May 1943) p. 230.

Pater? *Walter* Pater? Well, yes. Yes, well enough – after a fashion; that
fashion being of a kind somehow prone – I might say calculated – to
bring forth, to be conducive to, *legend*. Part of the legend survives in
there; the old lady, I mean, survives. She looks *cross*. I suspect she *is*
cross. May crossness explain her solitude?

I believe these two survivors had no second meeting.

NOTE

1. Walter Pater, influential writer on art and literature, had died in 1894.
Alice James's diary records an earlier encounter (8 May 1891) between James
and Miss Pater:

> Harry, yesterday, was calling at Mrs Humphry Ward's, who has just moved
> into a beautiful new house in Grosvenor Place, said to be one of the products of
> *Robert Elsmere*. Miss Pater was there also, and Harry looking over at the
> beautiful trees in Buckingham Palace Gardens was moved to address to her a
> lament over such a lost enjoyment in the heart of London, despised by the
> Queen and denied to the people; when she timorously said (with her eyes fixed
> upon them), 'Where are they?' H. said, 'Why, *there*: before your eyes!' To
> which she replied, 'Oh yes; I suppose they would be.' And this is a lady who is
> said by her accomplished family to be a 'mine of silent learning'. (*The Diary
> of Alice James*, p. 206)

The Genesis of *The Turn of the Screw** *

E. F. BENSON

Hopefully but sometimes ruefully did this family of young literary
aspirants try to follow [James] into his new manner, for there were no
more fervent worshippers than they of his earlier work. *Roderick Hudson*,
The Portrait of a Lady and such clear gems of story-telling. He had been
speaking to my mother about this change. 'All my earlier work was

* *As We Were* (London: Longmans, 1930) pp. 277–9.

subaqueous, subaqueous', he said, 'Now I have got my head, such as it is, above the water, such as it was.' One evening when he was staying with us at Addington, he and my father[1] lingered, talking together after tea, while we all drifted away to our various occupations, and though we heard no mention of the contents of that conversation at the time, there came of it an odd and interesting sequel. For, years later, Henry James wrote to my brother,[2] on the eve of the publication of the volume containing *The Turn of the Screw*, to the effect that the story had been told him on that occasion by my father. It is among the grimmest stories of the world, and, as has been noticed by more accomplished critics of his work than I, it has a singular directness and clarity which are not characteristic of Henry James at that period: the development and growing grip of the two speçtres which pervade it are singularly simple and uninvolved. Indeed the structure of it, apart from the actual style of the writing, is not like him, but if the bones and the blood of it were thus given him, the difference is easily accounted for: he followed definite lines. But the odd thing is that to all of us the story was absolutely new, and neither my mother nor my brother nor I had the faintest recollection of any tale of my father's which resembled it. The contents of the family story-box are usually fairly well known to the members of the circle, and it seems very improbable that we should all have forgotten so arresting a tale, if it was ever told to us. The whole incident is difficult to unravel, but Henry James was quite definite that my father told him this story, though in outline only, as having been one which he had been told in his youth, and he repeats the history of it in the preface he wrote to it, when it was republished in his collected edition. It is possible, of course, that my father merely gave him the barest hint for the story, saying what a shocking tale could be fashioned on the plot of two low ·and evil intelligences of the dead possessing themselves of the minds of two innocent children. That may have been enough to wind up Henry James's subconscious mind and set it ticking away, so that all but the barest basic idea was his. But in view of the simplicity of the narration, I am inclined to think that the gradual and gruesome approach of Peter Quint, from the time when he was first seen at the top of the tower down to his final assault and the tragic rescue of the boy's soul, was given him also.

NOTES

Edward Frederic Benson (1867–1940), novelist, was a brother of A. C. Benson (see p. 89). He was the third son of Edward White Benson (1829–96), who became Archbishop of Canterbury in 1882. The visit described here is recorded in James's notebook, which outlines the idea that developed into *The Turn of the Screw*, published in 1898 (see *The Notebooks of Henry James*, ed. F. O. Matthiessen and Kenneth B. Murdock (New York: Oxford University Press, 1947) pp. 178–9).

1. See above. E. W. Benson was a great admirer of James and quoted from *Roderick Hudson* in a sermon.

2. James's letter is dated 11 March 1898 and addressed to A. C. Benson (see *The Letters of Henry James*, ed. Percy Lubbock (New York: Scribner's, 1920) I, p. 263).

'Henry James at Dinner'*

ELIZABETH JORDAN

The most vivid memories I have of Henry James – and I have many – are connected with his habit of speech in his later years. Almost invariably he broke up his sentences into little groups of two, three, or four words, and repeated each group three times. In my autobiography I give an example of this which has persistently lingered with me because it was uttered by Mr James in the first conversation I ever had with him.

The scene was the London dinner table of Colonel and Mrs George Harvey[1] at Claridge's Hotel. Mr James and I had met that evening for the first time and he had taken me into dinner. That was in the early part of this century – about 1904, as I recall it – and I was much in awe of my escort. I had read all his books, but I had heard that socially he was very difficult.

He was nothing of the sort. He was smiling and chatty, and however he may have felt he had an engaging air of being interested. It was quite a large dinner, of twenty or twenty-four guests as I remember it, and one of our fellow guests was Henry Savage Landor, the explorer.[2] Mr Landor's experiences in Tibet, during which he was supposed to have been tortured by the natives whose forbidden city of Lhasa he had penetrated, were not many years behind him. Mr Landor was still willing to discuss them conversationally. He had done this so often in London, indeed, that I had met several leading Londoners who expressed to me the greatest doubts of the accuracy of Mr Landor's memories. On this occasion he

---

* 'Henry James at Dinner', *Mark Twain Quarterly*, V (Spring 1943) p. 7.

was well out of earshot at the other end of the long table, and I ventured to ask Mr James, who had evidently met him several times, whether he shared these doubts.

Mr James's reply has been the most popular of my social monologues ever since that occasion. I have always been careful, however, to display my little gift of imitation only to my family and most intimate friends. Colonel and Mrs George Harvey had heard this imitation and Colonel Harvey subsequently told Mr James about it and urged me to do it for him. There were only the Harveys, Mr James and myself in the room at the time. This was some months after my first meeting with Mr James and I felt that I knew him very well by that time, but I was naturally embarrassed at doing such a stunt.

Mr James took it magnificently, however, as I was pretty sure he would do. He roared with laughter and subsequently repeated the sentence himself to show the accuracy of the imitation. It was accurate, too. By that time I had caught the quality of his speaking voice as well as his accent, his emphasis, and his breath-control.

But here's the sentence, with marked explanations of tempo. We were speaking, you may remember, of Henry Savage Landor, and I had asked Mr James whether he shared the British doubts of Mr Landor's memory. This was his reply.

'Eliminating – ah – (very slow) eliminating – ah – eliminating nine-tenths – (faster) nine-tenths – nine-tenths of – of – of – of (very fast) what he claims (slower) of what he claims – of what he claims (very slow) there is still – there is still – there is still (very much faster) enough – left – e – nough left (slower) to make – to – make – to – make – a remarkable record (slow) a remark – able record, (slower) a remarkable record (very slow, with every word heavily emphasised).

My own explanation, as I gave it to Colonel and Mrs Harvey in the early stages of my acquaintance with Mr James, was that with his meticulous care in the choice of words, he was feeling for his words the first time, trying them out the second and accepting them and sending them forth as satisfactory the third time.

The most interesting phase of the habit was that he never changed a word. It was always exactly the right word in the beginning, as even Mr Henry James (incredibly modest for so great a man) had to admit to himself at the end.

NOTES

On Elizabeth Jordan, see p. 45. In her autobiography *Three Rousing Cheers* Elizabeth Jordan gives a shorter account of the same episode.

1. George Harvey was a wealthy American businessman who was president of Harper's, the publishing firm, and owned the *North American Review*. James stayed with him at his cottage at Deal Beach, New Jersey, when he visited America in 1904, the other guest on that occasion being Mark Twain. Harvey gave a dinner for James in New York in November of the same year; Twain was once more a guest.

2. H. S. Landor (grandson of the poet Walter Savage Landor) travelled extensively. He was the first white man to reach both sources of the Brahmaputra River. His book on Tibet was published in 1897.

James Has his Hair Cut*

J. M. BARRIE

. . . I had discovered another thing you can do in clubs, you can get your hair cut there. I naturally clung to that, but, alas, James, who was a true frequenter, clung to it also, and when one is swaddled in that white cloth one wants no friendly neighbour. At such times he and I conversed amiably from our chairs with raging breasts. Then one day I was in Manchester or Liverpool in a big hotel, and it came to me that now was my chance to get my hair cut in peace. I went downstairs, and just as they enveloped me in the loathly sheet I heard a groan from the adjoining chair and saw that its occupant was Henry James. After a moment, when anything might have happened, we both laughed despairingly, but I think with plucky sympathy, meaning that fate was too much for us. Later in the day we discussed the matter openly for the first time, but could come to no conclusion for future guidance. Each, however, without making any promise, did something to help. Feeling that I had been driven from society by its greatest ornament I let my hair go its own wild way, and he, though he remained in society, removed his beard, which was what had taken him so often to the salon of the artists. Not that I can claim the beard as a trophy of mine, but he did remove it about that time, and I should have been proud to be the shears, for the result was that at last his full face came into the open, and behold it was fair. One saw at last the lovely smile that had so long lain hidden in the forest.

No man of letters, I suppose, ever had a more disarming smile than

* *The Greenwood Hat* (London: Peter Davies, 1937) pp. 254–5.

his, and smiles, as I have told, are a subject about which I can speak with authority. It was worth losing a train (and sometimes you had to do that) while he rummaged for the right word. During the search the smile was playing about his face, a smile with which he was on such good terms that it was a part of him chuckling at the other parts of him. I remember once meeting him in the street and asking him how he liked a lecture we had both lately attended. I did not specially want to know nor he to tell, and as he sought for the right words it began to rain, and by and by it was raining heavily. In this predicament he signed to a passing growler and we got in and it remained there stationary until he reached the triumphant conclusion, which was that no one could have delivered a lecture with less offence. They certainly were absolutely the right words, but the smile's enjoyment while he searched for them was what I was watching. It brought one down like Leatherstocking's Killdeer.[1]

NOTE

J. M. (Sir James) Barrie (1860–1937), novelist and dramatist. He and James were both members of the Reform Club.

1. 'Leatherstocking' is the nickname of the hero of a series of novels by James Fenimore Cooper; 'Killdeer' is the name of his rifle.

James Wishes He Were Popular*

ALFRED SUTRO

Courteous and charming in his own magnificent, eighteenth-century fashion ... Henry James was a survival, or rather he belonged to a period of his own; he had his special grand manner, his own unostentatious dignity....

Henry James seldom unbent; he had no small talk, but his courtesy, the inherent charm of the man, pleased like rare wine. One night I was dining at the Garrick with W. W. Jacobs,[1] and at an adjoining table a

* *Celebrities and Simple Souls* (London: Duckworth, 1933) pp. 180–1, 182–3.

friend was entertaining Max Beerbohm[2] and Henry James. After dinner Jacobs and I went to their table for coffee, and I introduced Jacobs, whom Henry had never met. We sat and talked; suddenly James leant across and said, 'Mr Jacobs, I envy you.' 'You, Henry James, envy me!' cried Jacobs, always the most modest of men. James acknowledged the compliment with a graceful wave of the hand. 'Ah, Mr Jacobs,' he said, 'you are popular! Your admirable work is appreciated by a wide circle of readers; it has achieved popularity. Mine – never goes into a second edition. I should so much have loved to be popular!' I have, of course, paraphrased his words; I cannot attempt to reproduce the elegance of the diction, the pleasant rotundity of the sentence; but there was something curiously pathetic about the genuineness of this cry from the heart, and we were all of us impressed, and moved.

NOTES

Alfred Sutro (1863–1933), successful dramatist and translator of Maeterlinck.
1. W. W. Jacobs (1863–1943), popular writer of short stories.
2. See p. 139.

James at a Cricket Match*

REGINALD BLOMFIELD

It was at my cottage, Point Hill as it is called, that Henry James made the acquaintance of Rye. He took it in the months when we were not there, and was here year after year, tended by a devoted manservant,[1] whom we used to call Bardolph, after that rascal in Shakespeare whose 'nose would light a torch in hell'. Bardolph was devoted to his master and was much exercised about his health, because Henry James in those days used to go out on his bicycle and return in a state of complete deliquescence, for he was no athlete and quite unused to any form of active exercise; indeed, later on, when he had bought Lamb House, it was his custom to take the train to Hastings in the afternoons in order to get

* *Memoirs of an Architect* (London: Macmillan, 1932) pp. 94–5.

exercise by walking up and down the nice paved promenade. During our annual cricket weeks at Rye he used to come on to the ground, but he always used to sit in the tent talking to the ladies with his back to the cricket, probably thinking the game too absurd to be worth the attention of serious people. On the other hand, he used to subscribe to the cricket club, and my final impression of Henry James was that, though his brain was subtle enough when he had a pen in his hand, in the ordinary affairs of life he was just a kindly, generous innocent. He became so enamoured of Rye that he bought Lamb House and settled there. He used to come up and see us on Sunday afternoons, and his conversation was very interesting, in so far as one could follow his extremely involved sentences. I have an impression that I used to leave him on the terrace talking to somebody, while I had to go and arrange a set of lawn-tennis, and when I came back, found him still engaged on the sentence which he had begun before I left. He was a kind-hearted and sympathetic man, full of consideration for others, modest and even diffident considering his great and well-deserved reputation, and yet conscious of what was due to him. He once remarked to me on the occasion of an entertainment at Rye, at which in his opinion undue attention had been paid to a person of title, that it was 'a deplorable evening in every way'.

NOTE

Sir Reginald Blomfield (1856–1942) was a well-known architect; his work includes Lambeth Bridge, Swan and Edgar's in Piccadilly Circus, and the Carlton Club. He also published extensively on architectural history.

1. See p. 30, note 3.

Part IV

Life at Rye

'The Mayor-Elect of Rye'*

EDMUND GOSSE

His practice in regard to ... a visitor always was to descend to the railway station below the town to welcome the guest, who would instantly recognise his remarkable figure hurrying along the platform. Under the large soft hat would be visible the large pale face, anxiously scanning the carriage-windows and breaking into smiles of sunshine when the newcomer was discovered. Welcome was signified by both hands waved aloft, lifting the skirts of the customary cloak, like wings. Then, luggage attended to, and the arm of the guest securely seized, as though even now there might be an attempt at escape, a slow ascent on foot would begin up the steep streets, the last and steepest of all leading to a discreet door which admitted directly to the broad hall of Lamb House. Within were, to right and left, the pleasant old rooms, with low windows opening straight into the garden, which was so sheltered and economised as to seem actually spacious. Further to the left was a lofty detached room, full of books and lights, where in summer Henry James usually wrote, secluded from all possible disturbance. The ascent of arrival from the railway grew to be more and more interesting as time went on, and as the novelist became more and more a familiar and respected citizen it was much interrupted at last by bows from ladies and salaams from shopkeepers; many little boys and girls, the latter having often curtsied, had to be greeted and sometimes patted on the head. These social movements used to inspire in me the enquiry: 'Well, how soon are you to be the Mayor-Elect of Rye?' a pleasantry which was always well received. So obviously did Henry James, in the process of years, become the Leading Inhabitant that it grew to seem no impossibility. Stranger things had happened! No civic authority would have been more conscientious and few less efficient.

His outward appearance developed in accordance with his moral and intellectual expansion. I have said that in early life Henry James was not

* 'Henry James', *London Mercury*, II (1920) pp. 32–4.

'impressive'; as time went on his appearance became, on the contrary, excessively noticeable and arresting. He removed the beard which had long disguised his face, and so revealed the strong lines of mouth and chin, which responded to the majesty of the skull. In the breadth and smoothness of the head – Henry James became almost wholly bald early in life – there was at length something sacerdotal. As time went on, he grew less and less Anglo-Saxon in appearance and more Latin. I remember once seeing a Canon preaching in the Cathedral of Toulouse who was the picture of Henry James in his unction, his gravity, and his vehemence. Sometimes there could be noted – what Henry would have hated to think existing – a theatrical look which struck the eye, as though he might be some retired *jeune premier* of the Français, *jeune* no longer; and often the prelatical expression faded into a fleeting likeness to one or other celebrated Frenchman of letters (never to any Englishman or American), somewhat of Lacordaire in the intolerable scrutiny of the eyes, somewhat of Sainte-Beuve, too, in all except the mouth, which, though mobile and elastic, gave the impression in rest of being small. All these comparisons and suggestions, however, must be taken as the barest hints, intended to mark the tendency of Henry James's radically power-ful and unique outer appearance. The beautiful modelling of the brows, waxing and waning under the stress of excitement, is a point which singularly dwells in the memory.

It is very difficult to give an impression of his manner, which was complex in the extreme, now restrained with a deep reserve, now suddenly expanding, so as to leave the auditor breathless, into a flood of exuberance. He had the habit of keeping his friends apart from one another; his intimacies were contained in many watertight compart-ments. He disliked to think that he was the subject of an interchange of impressions, and though he who discussed everybody and everything with the most penetrating and analysing curiosity must have known perfectly well that he also, in his turn, was the theme of endless discussion, he liked to ignore it and to feign to be a bodiless spectator. Accordingly, he was not apt to pay for the revelations, confidences, guesses and what not which he so eagerly demanded and enjoyed by any coin of a similar species. He begged the human race to plunge into experiences, but he proposed to take no plunge himself, or at least to have no audience when he plunged.

So discreet was he, and so like a fountain sealed, that many of those who were well acquainted with him have supposed that he was mainly a creature of observation and fancy, and that life stirred his intellect while leaving his senses untouched. But every now and then he disclosed to a friend, or rather admitted such a friend to a flash or glimpse of deeper things. The glimpse was never prolonged or illuminated, it was like peering down for a moment through some chasm in the rocks dimmed by the vapour of a clash of waves. One such flash will always leave my memory dazzled. I was staying alone with Henry James at Rye one summer, and as twilight deepened we walked together in the garden. I forget by what meanders we approached the subject, but I suddenly found that in profuse and enigmatic language he was recounting to me an experience, something that had happened, not something repeated or imagined. He spoke of standing on the pavement of a city, in the dusk, and of gazing upwards across the misty street, watching, watching for the lighting of a lamp in a window on the third storey. And the lamp blazed out, and through bursting tears he strained to see what was behind it, the unapproachable face. And for hours he stood there, wet with the rain, brushed by the phantom hurrying figures of the scene, and never from behind the lamp was for one moment visible the face. The mysterious and poignant revelation closed, and one could make no comment, ask no question, being throttled oneself by an overpowering emotion. And for a long time Henry James shuffled beside me in the darkness, shaking the dew off the laurels, and still there was no sound at all in the garden but what our heels made crunching the gravel, nor was the silence broken when suddenly we entered the house and he disappeared for an hour.

NOTE

On Gosse, see p. 10.

James at Home*

MRS J. T. FIELDS

Monday, 13 September 1898. We left London about 11 o'clock for Rye, to pass the day with Mr Henry James. He was waiting for us at the station

* M. A. DeWolfe Howe, *Memories of a Hostess* (Boston, Mass.: Atlantic Monthly Press, 1922) pp. 297–300.

with a carriage, and in five minutes we found ourselves at the top of a silent little winding street, at a green door with a brass knocker, wearing the air of impenetrable respectability which is so well known in England. Another instant and an old servant, Smith (who with his wife has been in Mr James's service for twenty years), opened the door and helped us from the carriage. It was a pretty interior – large enough for elegance, and simple enough to suit the severe taste of a scholar and private gentleman.

Mr James was intent on the largest hospitality. We were asked upstairs over a staircase with a pretty balustrade and plain green drugget on the steps; everything was of the severest plainness, but in the best taste, 'not at all austere', as he himself wrote us.

We soon went down again after leaving our hats, to find a young gentleman, Mr McAlpine,[1] who is Mr James's secretary, with him, awaiting us. This young man is just the person to help Mr James. He has a bump of reverence and appreciates his position and opportunity. We sat in the parlour opening on a pretty garden for some time, until Mr James said he could not conceive why luncheon was not ready and he must go and inquire, which he did in a very responsible manner, and soon after Smith appeared to announce the feast. Again a pretty room and table. We enjoyed our talk together sincerely at luncheon and afterward strolled into the garden. The dominating note was dear Mr James's pleasure in having a home of his own to which he might ask us. From the garden, of course, we could see the pretty old house still more satisfactorily. An old brick wall concealed by vines and laurels surrounds the whole irregular domain; a door from the garden leads into a paved courtyard which seemed to give Mr James peculiar satisfaction; returning to the garden, and on the other side, at an angle with the house, is a building which he laughingly called the temple of the Muse. This is his own place *par excellence*. A good writing-table and one for his secretary, a typewriter, books, and a sketch by Du Maurier, with a few other pictures (rather mementoes than works of art), excellent windows with clear light, such is the temple! Evidently an admirable spot for his work.

After we returned to the parlour Mr James took occasion to tell Sarah[2] how deeply and sincerely he appreciated her work; how he rereads it with increasing admiration. . . .

NOTES

The extract is taken from the diary of Mrs James T. Fields of Boston. James had frequented her literary salon during his youth; her husband, as editor of the

Atlantic Monthly, had published some of his early work. After her visit to Rye, James wrote in a letter to Mrs Humphry Ward that 'Mrs Fields took me back to my far-away youth and *hers* – when she was so pretty and I was so aspiring.'

1. William McAlpine was a young Scot whom James engaged as a part-time stenographer in February 1897 as a result of the pains in his right wrist (presumably a form of writer's cramp) that he suffered during the composition of *What Maisie Knew*. McAlpine was at first employed to take down James's letters in shorthand; but soon James was dictating both his letters and his fiction to be taken down directly on the typewriter, and he continued this practice. As he wrote to one correspondent, 'I can address you only through an embroidered veil of sound'.

2. Mrs Fields was accompanied by Sarah Orne Jewett (1849–1909), American authoress, best remembered for her stories and sketches of rural life in New England. For James's reaction to reading her *Tales of New England* in 1899, see *The Notebooks of Henry James*, p. 286.

A Visit to Lamb House (January 1900)*

A. C. BENSON

Henry James, looking somewhat cold, tired and old, met me at the station: most affectionate, patting me on the shoulder and really welcoming with abundance of *petits soins*.

The town stands on a steep sort of island, rising from the great sea-plain. Inland it is separated from hilly country by one valley only; but south and south-east the flat plain stretches like a green chessboard for miles. You see the winding stream, very pale in the sunset, the shipyards, the houses of Rye Harbour, the strand dotted with Martello towers, the wooded heights of Winchelsea, the great ocean-steamers passing up and down channel, and the great green expanse of Romney Marsh.

The town is incredibly picturesque. It has a mouldering castle, a great gateway, a huge church like a cathedral, a few gabled and timbered cottages – but for the most part is built of wholesome Georgian brick,

* *The Diary of Arthur Christopher Benson*, ed. Percy Lubbock (New York: Longmans, Green, 1926) pp. 46–8.

with fine mouldings, good doorhoods, and with an air of Dutch trimness and bourgeois stateliness, like a cathedral town, which breathes tranquillity. We walked slowly up, and came to Lamb House. It is sober red Georgian; facing you as you come up is the bow-window of the garden-house with all its white casements – used by H. J. to write in in summer. The house has a tall door, strangely fortified inside by bolts, admitting into a white panelled hall. There are three small panelled sitting-rooms, besides the dining-room. The place has been carefully done up, and is very clean, trim, precise, but all old and harmonious. . . .

Dined simply at 7.30, with many apologies from H. J. about the fare. . . . He was full of talk, though he looked weary, often passing his hand over his eyes; but he refined and defined, was intricate, magniloquent, rhetorical, humorous, not so much like a talker, but like a writer repeating his technical processes aloud – like a savant working out a problem. He told me a long story about Heinemann, and spoke with hatred of the business and the monetary side of art. He evidently thinks that *art* is nearly dead among English writers – no criticism, no instinct for what is good. . . . He talked of Mrs Oliphant, Carlyle – whatever I began. 'I had not read a *line* that the poor woman had written for *years* – not for years; and when she died, Henley[1] – do you know him, the rude, boisterous, windy, headstrong Henley? – Henley, as I say, said to me, "Have you read *Kirsteen?*"[2] I replied that as a matter of fact, no – h'm – I had not read it. Henley said, 'That you should have any pretensions to interest in literature and should dare to say that you have not read *Kirsteen!*' I took my bludgeoning patiently and humbly, my dear Arthur – went back and read it, and was at once confirmed, after twenty pages, in my belief – I laboured through the book – that the poor soul had a simply *feminine* conception of literature, down-at-heel work – buffeting along like a ragged creature in a high wind, and just struggling to the goal, and falling in a quivering mass of faintness and fatuity. Yes, no doubt she was a gallant woman – though with no species of wisdom – but an artist, an artist – !' He held his hands up and stared woefully at me. . . .

H. J. works hard; he establishes me in a little high-walled white parlour, very comfortable, but is full of fear that I am unhappy. He comes in, pokes the fire, presses a cigarette on me, puts his hand on my shoulder, looks inquiringly at me, and hurries away. His eyes are *piercing*. To see him, when I came down to breakfast this morning, in a kind of Holbein square cap of velvet and black velvet coat, scattering bread on the frozen lawn to the birds, was delightful. . . .

We lunched together with his secretary, a young Scot.[3] H. J. ate little, rolled his eyes, waited on us, walked about, talked – finally hurried me off

for a stroll before my train. All his instincts are of a kind that make me
feel vulgar – his consideration, hospitality, care of arrangement,
thoughtfulness.... He seemed to know everyone to speak to – an elderly
clergyman in a pony-carriage, a young man riding. Three nice-looking
girls met us, two of fourteen and fifteen, and a little maid of seven or
eight, who threw herself upon H. J. with cooing noises of delight and
kissed him repeatedly and effusively, the dogs also bounding up to him.
He introduced me with great gravity.... We got to the station; he said an
affectionate farewell, pressing me to come again; I went away refreshed,
stimulated, sobered, and journeyed under a dark and stormy sky to the
dreary and loathsome town of Hastings.

NOTES

Arthur Christopher Benson (1862–1925) taught at Eton and later became
Fellow and subsequently Master of Magdalene College, Cambridge. He belonged to a prominent family (his father was Archbishop of Canterbury) and his
brothers E. F. Benson and R. H. Benson were both authors (on the former, see
p. 73). A. C. Benson himself published many very successful but now forgotten
books and was in addition a compulsive diarist; his diary, running to nearly five
million words, includes candid impressions of many of the literary figures of his
generation. The selections published by Percy Lubbock in 1926 contain many
omissions and some inaccuracies. See David Newsome, *On the Edge of Paradise*
(London: John Murray, 1980).
  For Benson's accounts of James's conversation, see pp. 120–5.
  1. W. E. Henley (1848–1903), poet and editor.
  2. Margaret Oliphant, prolific and popular novelist, died in 1897. Her novel
Kirsteen had appeared in 1890.
  3. William McAlpine: see p. 87.

'Genial Nebulosity'*

E. F. BENSON

He was soaked and saturated in the creation and criticism of literature:
they permeated his being, an organic part of it. Friends and literature
were his passions, and when he talked to a friend the most trivial incident

* *Final Edition* (London: Longmans, 1940) pp. 3–6.

must be dipped in style, as in Tyrian dye: he put what he wanted to say in a chiselled casket of words. One day he paid a call on a neighbour in Rye and he wished to tell us that when the door was opened to his ring a black dog appeared on the threshold. But he could not bring himself to say 'black dog', for that would have been a scarcely decent *déshabillé* for his information. 'And from the dusky entry,' he said, 'there emerged something black, something canine.' And below that formal and entrancing talk stirred the spell of his geniality and benevolence, of his absorbed interest in all the qualities, rich and poor, of humanity. He disliked certain of these with singular intensity; anything approaching rudeness or inquisitiveness was abhorrent to him, rousing in him just such a sense of sickened pity as he felt for the work of poor Mrs Oliphant.[1] On the other hand he treasured and fondled all that responded to his fastidious instincts and to his affection. 'I am singularly accessible,' he wrote, 'to all demonstrations of regard.' An unfriendly deed or word on the part of one whom he had treated as a friend was final. He did not want even to see him again.

One afternoon I played golf at Camber. Beyond the links in those days extended the stretch of tussocked dunes bordered by shining sands, which now is covered with a confluent rash of small perky bungalows and bathing-suits hung up to dry, and is resonant with motor-cycles and loud speakers. He met us after our game at the clubhouse and gave us tea, in an ecstasy of genial nebulosity as to what we had been doing. 'Some be-flagged jam pots, I understand, my dear Fred, let into the soil at long but varying distances. A swoop, a swing, a flourish of steel, a dormy': and he wrote to Arthur [Benson] saying that he thought I put golf too high among intellectual pursuits. On other afternoons we walked very slowly with frequent pauses for salutations to his friends, a child, a station-master, or a dog, for each of whom he had some special word, through the cobbled streets of the town and out on to the levels of the sheep-grazed marsh, with the sky above enormous as at sea.

I do not think he took much notice of the aspects of nature; he was scarcely more conscious of them than is a man, deep in thought, of the comfort of the arm-chair in which he sits. Nature, at any rate, only appealed to him fitfully, as the cool water and the plane-trees of the Ilyssus momentarily diverted the attention of Socrates from his philosophy and his Phaedrus, till at the end of their talk he invoked Pan and the deities who haunted the place to give him and his companion inward beauty of soul. Of all men that I have ever met he was the most Socratic – his mind was always occupied within on its own surmises and speculations. In the middle of light superficial talk it withdrew itself into depths of the element in which it functioned, like a diving submarine. . . .

He laughed but little, but he was as full of humour as the packed portmanteau, 'beautifully creaking'. In these distant memories I recall his story of how on his way down to the High Street, he saw advancing towards him a woman whom he knew that he knew, but whom his racked memory failed to identify. As they drew fatally nearer each other, she made a bee-line for him across the roadway, and, still unidentified, opened conversation. 'I've had the rest of it,' she said, 'made into rissoles.' Recognition followed at once. 'And then in fact,' he said, 'the cudgelling of my brain ceased, for I recognised my own cook and knew that she was speaking of the leg of lamb I had eaten hot and roast on Monday and cold on Tuesday.'

NOTE

On E. F. Benson, see p. 73. Benson himself later lived in Lamb House.
  1. See p. 89.

'I Have Lost Touch with my Own People'*

HAMLIN GARLAND

He was curious about conditions of authorship in America – wanted to know more of the men whose books sold so enormously. He was amazed at my statement of the money certain writers made by their writings. He had no understanding of the midland America. Chicago was almost as alien to him as a landscape on Mars. He resented the self-satisfaction of the novelists who sold their hundreds of thousands of copies of superficial fiction. 'I have never even heard of them', he said when I named two of the most successful. . . .

He spoke of the placid quiet of his little town, of his kindly neighbours. 'They are a great comfort to me, for I am a lonely man', he said. He spoke

* *Roadside Meetings* (London: John Lane, 1931) pp. 459–65.

rejoicingly of the fact that there were only three wheeled vehicles in the village. 'You noticed, perhaps, that the streets are grass-grown between the cobbles? Only now and then do I hear a footfall pass my door.'

He alluded gracefully to my letters of appreciation of his stories. 'I have for many years discharged my books into America as into a hollow void,' he admitted with sombre inflection; 'no word but yours has lately come back to me.'

No doubt this was an exaggeration, and yet he meant that I should remember it as a confession.

He spoke of Howells with sincere love and appreciation. 'He is an artist – always – but he has written too much, and so have I.'

I then quoted Howells's remark, apropos of this criticism: 'But what else am I to do?'

James instantly agreed. 'Yes, we writers are lost without our pens in our hands.'

He praised Owen Wister's[1] work and commended Mrs Wharton's *Valley of Decision*,[2] and this led up to his own fervid enthusiasm for Italy. He advised my hastening there at once. 'Why study France?' he demanded; 'France is only an imitation of Italy. Why waste time on the imitation when you can see the real thing?'

Precisely what he meant by this I could not determine, but I took it to mean that the historical remains of France were Roman. He could not have meant that France was in any modern sense an imitation of Italy.

A little farther on he spoke of his novel *The Ambassadors* as the best of all he had written. 'I am rewriting, not merely revising, my earlier books', he explained, and to this I could not respond with any enthusiasm. . . .

He referred to Thomas Hardy as a man who had lost his power. Of his brother William James he spoke with affection. Several other American writers came in for his comment, which was never bitter nor ironic. He had a certain straightforward glance which made his words sound less harsh than they would look if printed. As he described his New York ancestry, I perceived that he was less remote than he had seemed to me hitherto. 'I still read the New York journals and keep informed of New World politics in the mass!' he said.

He became very much in earnest at last and said something which surprised and gratified me. It was an admission I had not expected him to make. 'If I were to live my life over again,' he said in a low voice, and fixing upon me a sombre glance, 'I would be an American. I would steep myself in America, I would know no other land. I would study its beautiful side. The mixture of Europe and America which you see in me has proved disastrous. It has made of me a man who is neither American nor European. I have lost touch with my own people, and I live here alone.[3] My neighbours are friendly, but they are not of my blood, except remotely. As a man grows old he feels these conditions more than when he is young. I shall never return to the United States, but I wish I could.' . . .

After our tea, which was served on a little table out under the trees, he took me to see the town, pointing out the most ancient of the buildings, well knowing that as a man from the plains of Iowa I would be interested in age-worn walls and door sills. He took me to the Old Mermaid Tavern, in which was a marvellous fireplace, as wide as the end of the room itself, with benches at the corners. Everybody we met seemed to know and like him; whether they recognised in him a famous author or not I cannot tell, but they certainly regarded him as a good neighbour. He greeted every one we met most genially. He was on terms with the postman and the butcher's boy. There was nothing austere or remote in his bearing. On the contrary, he had the air of a curate making the rounds of his village.

At seven o'clock we dined in his exquisite little dining room, and the dinner, which came on quite formally, was delicious. He had no other guest, but he presided at the service end of the table with quiet formality. The mahogany glistened with the care which had been lavished upon it, the silver was interesting and beautiful, and the walls of the room tasteful and cheerful – and yet I could not keep out of my mind a picture of him sitting here alone, as he confessed he did on many, many nights. To grow old even with your children all about you is a sorrowful business, but to grow old in a land filled with strangers is sadder still.

It was late when I went to bed that night, my mind filled with literary and artistic problems called up by his profound comment. The questions of National art, of Realism and Idealism, of New World garishness and crudeness, of its growing power and complexity – these were among the matters we had discussed. That James lived on the highest plane of life and thought was evident. He had no distractions, no indulgences. He permitted himself no loafing, no relaxation. He had not even the comfort of a comic spirit such as Clemens[4] had. He was in earnest all the time – a genial earnestness, but an earnestness which could not be diverted. . . .

We breakfasted in such comfort, so simple but so perfect as to form the most delightful luxury. The sun shone in at our window, the silver gleamed cheerily, the coffee was delicious, and James, immaculately clad and fresh and rosy again, presided at the opposite side of the table while his miraculous servants attended us.

At the close of our meal I said, 'It is your habit to work in the morning – that I know, and I want you to keep to your routine. Don't permit me to interrupt your morning task.'

'Very well,' he said. 'I will take you at your word, but first I want you to see my workshop.'

His 'shop' was a small detached building standing in the corner of the garden, and in the large room littered with books and manuscripts I found a smart young woman stenographer at work. James showed me the changes he was making in his earlier books – work which I did not approve, for he was rewriting these stories. In my judgement he was not bettering them; on the contrary it seemed to me he was transforming them into something which was neither of the past nor of the present. I think he was now aware of my disapproval, for he went on to explain that he found in the early versions many crudities which he could not think of allowing the future to observe – 'if people ever take the trouble to look into my books', he added, with a note of melancholy in his voice.

After giving me elaborate directions concerning other landmarks of the region, he suddenly said, 'But why should I not be your guide again? You do not come often. My work can wait.'

My protesting availed nothing. Putting his secretary at another task he told me to come with him. 'There are some other houses which I must show you. They are owned by some friends of mine and they will be glad to let you have a glimpse of them.'

As he led me about the town, discovering for me delightful Georgian types of dwellings, the people everywhere greeted him with smiling cordiality. They liked and honoured him, that was evident, and it gave me a keen sense of satisfaction to find him more and more neighbourly, taking an interest in what his fellow citizens were doing and thinking. This phase of him was as surprising as it was amusing. To hear him asking after a child's health, or inquiring when Mr Brown would return from London, was a revelation of the fact that, after all, he was more than half New England.

He sped me on my way to France with a hearty invitation to come and see him on my return, and I particularly urged him to come again to America, in order that we might show him the honour which so many of us were eager to pay, and also in order that we might profit by his criticism. To this he replied very thoughtfully, 'I may do so, but I fear I shall not get so far as Chicago.'

NOTES

Hamlin Garland (1860–1940) was an American novelist and historian. He attended a dinner given for James in New York by Colonel George Harvey in November 1904, and James dined with him when he visited Chicago in 1905.

Garland spent a night as James's guest at Lamb House, Rye, in June 1906, and it is presumably to this visit that the passage refers.

Garland's diary provides a picture of James during his visit to Chicago:

He has forgotten many of his books and spoke of them rather vaguely as though they represented another phase on various planes of his life. He has lost his enthusiasms but still has his intellectual interests. He is going on now out of sheer momentum. Chicago people have seemed very remote to him and aside from his visit to Taft's studio he met only such people and their friends. (Quoted in *Master*, p. 290)

1. Owen Wister (1860–1938), American author.
2. Edith Wharton's novel had been published in 1902.
3. Leon Edel has commented as follows on Garland's version of this conversation:

This has been read by many as Henry James's acknowledgement that his expatriation was a large mistake. Garland's notebook of the time shows however that James did not speak as positively. It has him saying, 'if I were to live my life again I would be American – steep myself in it – know no other'. He then added that the 'mixture of Europe and America is disastrous' – so Garland originally noted – but he did not use the words 'which you see in me'. These were inserted by Garland. (*Master*, p. 320)

4. Samuel Langhorne Clemens (1835–1910), better known as Mark Twain. For his meetings with James, see p. 76.

James at Work*

THEODORA BOSANQUET

He asked no questions at that interview about my speed on a typewriter or about anything else. The friend to whom he had applied for an amanuensis had told him that I was sufficiently the right young woman for his purpose and he relied on her word. He had, at the best, little hope of any young woman beyond docility. We sat in armchairs on either side of a fireless grate while we observed each other. I suppose he found me harmless and I know that I found him overwhelming. He was much more massive than I had expected, much broader and stouter and stronger. I remembered that someone had told me he used to be taken for

* *Henry James at Work* (London: Hogarth Press, 1924) pp. 244–55, 264–8.

a sea-captain when he wore a beard, but it was clear that now, with the beard shaved away, he would hardly have passed for, say, an admiral, in spite of the keen grey eyes set in a face burned to a colourable sea-faring brown by the Italian sun. No successful naval officer could have afforded to keep that sensitive mobile mouth. After the interview I wondered what kind of impression one might have gained from a chance encounter in some such observation cell as a railway carriage. Would it have been possible to fit him confidently into any single category? He had reacted with so much success against both the American accent and the English manner that he seemed only doubtfully Anglo-Saxon. He might perhaps have been some species of disguised cardinal, or even a Roman noble-man amusing himself by playing the part of a Sussex squire. The observer could at least have guessed that any part he chose to assume would be finely conceived and generously played, for his features were all cast in the classical mould of greatness. He might very well have been a merciful Cæsar or a benevolent Napoleon, and a painter who worked at his portrait a year or two later was excusably reminded of so many illustrious makers of history that he declared it to be a hard task to isolate the individual character of the model.

If the interview was overwhelming, it had none of the usual awkward-ness of such curious conversations. Instead of critical angles and discon-certing silences, there were only benign curves and ample reassurances. There was encouraging gaiety in an expanse of bright check waistcoat. He invited me to ask any questions I liked, but I had none to ask. I wanted nothing but to be allowed to go to Rye and work his typewriter. He was prepared, however, with his statements and, once I was seated opposite to him, the strong, slow stream of his deliberate speech played over me without ceasing. He had it on his mind to tell me the conditions of life and labour at Rye, and he unburdened himself fully, with numberless amplifications and qualifications but without any real break. It would be a dull business, he warned me, and I should probably find Rye a dull place. He told me of rooms in Mermaid Street, 'very simple, rustic and antique – but that is the case for everything near my house, and this particular little old house is very near mine, and I know the good woman for kind and worthy and a convenient cook and in short——'. It was settled at once that I should take the rooms, that I should begin my duties in October.

*   *   *

Since winter was approaching, Henry James had begun to use a panelled, green-painted room on the upper floor of Lamb House for his work. It was known simply as the green room. It had many advantages as a winter workroom, for it was small enough to be easily warmed and a wide south window caught all the morning sunshine. The window overhung the smooth, green lawn, shaded in summer by a mulberry tree, surrounded by roses and enclosed behind a tall, brick wall. It never failed to give the owner pleasure to look out of this window at his charming English garden where he could watch his English gardener digging the flowerbeds or mowing the lawn or sweeping up fallen leaves. There was another window for the afternoon sun, looking towards Winchelsea and doubly glazed against the force of the westerly gales. Three high bookcases, two big writing-desks and an easy chair filled most of the space in the green room, but left enough clear floor for a restricted amount of the pacing exercise that was indispensable to literary composition. On summer days Henry James liked better to work in the large 'garden room' which gave him a longer stretch for perambulation and a window overlooking the cobbled street that curved up the hill past his door. He liked to be able to relieve the tension of a difficult sentence by a glance down the street; he enjoyed hailing a passing friend or watching a motor-car pant up the sharp little slope. The sight of one of these vehicles could be counted on to draw from him a vigorous outburst of amazement, admiration, or horror for the complications of an age that produced such efficient monsters for gobbling protective distance.

The business of acting as a medium between the spoken and the typewritten word was at first as alarming as it was fascinating. The most handsome and expensive typewriters exercise as vicious an influence as any others over the spelling of the operator, and the new pattern of a Remington machine which I found installed offered a few additional problems. But Henry James's patience during my struggles with that baffling mechanism was unfailing – he watched me helplessly, for he was one of the few men without the smallest pretension to the understanding of a machine – and he was as easy to spell from as an open dictionary. The experience of years had evidently taught him that it was not safe to leave any word of more than one syllable to luck. He took pains to pronounce every pronounceable letter, he always spelt out words which the ear might confuse with others, and never left a single punctuation mark unuttered, except sometimes that necessary point, the full stop. Occasionally, in a low 'aside' he would interject a few words for the enlightenment of the amanuensis, adding, for instance, after spelling out 'The Newcomes', that the words were the title of a novel by one Thackeray.

The practice of dictation was begun in the nineties. By 1907 it was a confirmed habit, its effects being easily recognisable in his style, which

became more and more like free, involved, unanswered talk. 'I know,' he
once said to me, 'that I'm too diffuse when I'm dictating.' But he found
dictation not only easier but a more inspiring method of composing than
writing with his own hand, and he considered that the gain in expression
more than compensated for any loss of concision. The spelling out of the
words, the indication of commas, were scarcely felt as a drag on the
movement of his thought. 'It all seems,' he once explained, 'to be so
much more effectively and unceasingly *pulled* out of me in speech than in
writing.' Indeed, at the time when I began to work for him, he had
reached a stage at which the click of a Remington machine acted as a
positive spur. He found it more difficult to compose to the music of any
other make. During a fortnight when the Remington was out of order he
dictated to an Oliver typewriter with evident discomfort, and he found it
almost impossibly disconcerting to speak to something that made no
responsive sound at all. Once or twice when he was ill and in bed I took
down a note or two by hand, but as a rule he liked to have the typewriter
moved into his bedroom for even the shortest letters. Yet there were to
the end certain kinds of work which he was obliged to do with a pen.
Plays, if they were to be kept within the limits of possible performance,
and short stories, if they were to remain within the bounds of publication
in a monthly magazine, must be written by hand. He was well aware that
the manual labour of writing was his best aid to a desired brevity. The
plays – such a play as *The Outcry*,[1] for instance – were copied straight
from his manuscript, since he was too much afraid of 'the murderous
limits of the English theatre' to risk the temptation of dictation and
embroidery. With the short stories he allowed himself a little more
freedom, dictating them from his written draft and expanding them as he
went to an extent which inevitably defeated his original purpose. It is
almost literally true to say of the sheaf of tales collected in *The Finer
Grain*[2] that they were all written in response to a single request for a short
story for *Harper's Monthly Magazine*. The length was to be about 5000
words and each promising idea was cultivated in the optimistic belief
that it would produce a flower too frail and small to demand any
exhaustive treatment. But even under pressure of being written by hand,
with dictated interpolations rigidly restricted, each in turn pushed out to
lengths that no chopping could reduce to the word limit. The tale
eventually printed was *Crapy Cornelia*,[3] but, although it was the shortest
of the batch, it was thought too long to be published in one number and
appeared in two sections, to the great annoyance of the author.

*   *   *

The method adopted for full-length novels was very different. With a clear run of 100,000 words or more before him, Henry James always cherished the delusive expectation of being able to fit his theme quite easily between the covers of a volume. It was not until he was more than half way through that the problem of space began to be embarrassing. At the beginning he had no questions of compression to attend to, and he 'broke ground', as he said, by talking to himself day by day about the characters and construction until the persons and their actions were vividly present to his inward eye. This soliloquy was of course recorded on the typewriter. He had from far back tended to dramatise all the material that life gave him, and he more and more prefigured his novels as staged performances, arranged in acts and scenes, with the characters making their observed entrances and exits. These scenes he worked out until he felt himself so thoroughly possessed of the action that he could begin on the dictation of the book itself – a process which has been incorrectly described by one critic as redictation from a rough draft. . . .

The preliminary sketch was seldom consulted after the novel began to take permanent shape, but the same method of 'talking out' was resorted to at difficult points of the narrative as it progressed, always for the sake of testing in advance the values of the persons involved in a given situation, so that their creator should ensure their right action both for the development of the drama and the truth of their relations to each other. The knowledge of all the conscious motives and concealments of his creatures, gained by unwearied observation of their attitudes behind the scenes, enabled Henry James to exhibit them with a final confidence that dispensed with explanations. Among certain stumbling blocks in the path of the perfect comprehension of his readers is their uneasy doubt of the sincerity of the conversational encounters recorded. Most novelists provide some clue to help their readers to distinguish truth from falsehood, and in the theatre, although husbands and wives may be deceived by lies, the audience is usually privy to the plot. But a study of the Notes to *The Ivory Tower* will make it clear that between the people created by Henry James lying is as frequent as among mortals and not any easier to detect.

For the volumes of memories, *A Small Boy and Others, Notes of a Son and Brother*, and the uncompleted *Middle Years*, no preliminary work was needed. A straight dive into the past brought to the surface treasure after treasure, a wealth of material which became embarrassing. The earlier book was begun in 1911, after Henry James had returned from a year in the United States, where he had been called by his brother's fatal illness. He had come back, after many seasons of country solitude, to his former love of the friendly London winter, and for the first few months after his return from America he lodged near the Reform Club and came to the old house in Chelsea where I was living and where he had taken a room for his work. It was a quiet room, long and narrow and rather dark – he used to speak of it as 'my Chelsea cellar'. There he settled down to write what, as he outlined it to me, was to be a set of notes to his brother William's early letters, prefaced by a brief account of the family into which they were both born. But an entire volume of memories was finished before bringing William to an age for writing letters, and *A Small Boy* came to a rather abrupt end as a result of the writer's sudden decision that a break must be made at once if the flood of remembrance was not to drown his pious intention.

It was extraordinarily easy for him to recover the past; he had always been sensitive to impressions and his mind was stored with records of exposure. All he had to do was to render his sense of those records as adequately as he could. Each morning, after reading over the pages written the day before, he would settle down in a chair for an hour or so of conscious effort. Then, lifted on a rising tide of inspiration, he would get up and pace up and down the room, sounding out the periods in tones of resonant assurance. At such times he was beyond reach of irrelevant sounds or sights. Hosts of cats – a tribe he usually routed with shouts of execration – might wail outside the window, phalanxes of motor-cars bearing dreaded visitors might hoot at the door. He heard nothing of them. The only thing that could arrest his progress was the escape of the word he wanted to use. When that had vanished he broke off the rhythmic pacing and made his way to a chimney-piece or book-case tall enough to support his elbows while he rested his head in his hands and audibly pursued the fugitive.

*   *   *

In the summer of 1907, when I began to tap the Remington typewriter at Henry James's dictation, he was engaged on the arduous task of preparing his Novels and Tales for the definitive New York Edition, published in 1909. Since it was only between breakfast and luncheon that he undertook what he called 'inventive' work, he gave the hours from half-past ten to half-past one to the composition of the prefaces which are so interesting a feature of the edition. In the evenings he read over again the work of former years, treating the printed pages like so many proof-sheets of extremely corrupt text. The revision was a task he had seen in advance as formidable. He had cultivated the habit of forgetting past achievements almost to the pitch of a sincere conviction that nothing he had written before about 1890 could come with any shred of credit through the ordeal of a critical inspection. On a morning when he was obliged to give time to the selection of a set of tales for a forthcoming volume, he confessed that the difficulty of selection was mainly the difficulty of reading them at all. 'They seem', he said, 'so bad until I *have* read them that I can't force myself to go through them except with a pen in my hand, altering as I go the crudities and ineptitudes that to my sense deform each page.' Unfamiliarity and adverse prejudice are rare advantages for a writer to bring to the task of choosing among his works. For Henry James the prejudice might give way to half reluctant appreciation as the unfamiliarity passed into recognition, but it must be clear to every reader of the prefaces that he never lost the sense of being paternally responsible for two distinct families. For the earlier brood, acknowledged fruit of his alliance with Romance, he claimed indulgence on the ground of their youthful spontaneity, their confident assurance, their rather touching good faith. One catches echoes of a plea that these elderly youngsters may not be too closely compared, to their inevitable disadvantage, with the richly endowed, the carefully bred, the highly civilised and sensitised children of his second marriage, contracted with that wealthy bride, Experience. Attentive readers of the novels may perhaps find the distinction between these two groups less remarkable than it seemed to their writer. They may even wonder whether the second marriage was not rather a silver wedding, with the old romantic mistress cleverly disguised as a woman of the world. The different note was possibly due more to the substitution of dictation for pen and ink than to any profound change of heart. But whatever the reason, their author certainly found it necessary to spend a good deal of time working on the earlier tales before he considered them fit for appearance in the company of those composed later. Some members of the elder family he entirely cast off, not counting them worth the expense of completely new clothes. Others he left in their place more from a necessary, though deprecated, respect for the declared taste of the reading public than because he loved them for their own sake. It would, for instance, have been difficult to exclude *Daisy Miller* from any representative collection of his work, yet the popularity of the tale had become almost a grievance. To be acclaimed as the author of *Daisy Miller* by persons blandly unconscious of *The Wings of the Dove* or *The Golden Bowl* was a reason among many for Henry James's despair of intelligent comprehension. Confronted repeatedly with *Daisy*, he felt himself rather in the position of some *grande dame* who, with a jewel-case of sparkling diamonds, is constrained by her admirers always to appear in the simple string of moonstones worn at her first dance.

From the moment he began to read over the earlier tales, he found

himself involved in a highly practical examination of the scope and limits
of permissible revision. Poets, as he pointed out, have often revised their
verse with good effect. Why should the novelist not have equal licence?
The only sound reason for not altering anything is a conviction that it
cannot be improved. It was Henry James's profound conviction that he
could improve his early writing in nearly every sentence. Not to revise
would have been to confess to a loss of faith in himself, and it was not
likely that the writer who had fasted for forty years in the wilderness of
British and American misconceptions without yielding a scrap of intellectual integrity to editorial or publishing tempters should have lost faith
in himself. But he was well aware that the game of revision must be
played with a due observance of the rules. He knew that no novelist can
safely afford to repudiate his fundamental understanding with his
readers that the tale he has to tell is at least as true as history and the
figures he has set in motion at least as independently alive as the people
we see in offices and motor-cars. . . .

★   ★   ★

Many men whose prime business is the art of writing find rest and
refreshment in other occupations. They marry or they keep dogs, they
play golf or bridge, they study Sanskrit or collect postage stamps. Except
for a period of ownership of a dachshund, Henry James did none of these
things. He lived a life consecrated to the service of a jealous, insatiable,
and supremely rewarding goddess, and all his activities had essential
reference to that service. He had a great belief in the virtues of air and
exercise, and he was expert at making a walk of two or three miles last for
as many hours by his habit of punctuating movement with frequent and
prolonged halts for meditation or conversation. He liked the exhilaration
of driving in a motor-car, which gave him, he said, 'a sense of spiritual
adventure'. He liked a communicative companion. Indeed the cultiva-
tion of friendships may be said to have been his sole recreation. To the
very end of his life he was quick to recognise every chance of forming a
friendly relation, swift to act on his recognition, and beautifully ready to
protect and nourish the warm life of engendered affection. His letters,
especially those written in his later years, are more than anything else
great generous gestures of remembrance, gathering up and embracing
his correspondents much as his talk would gather up his hearers and
sweep them along on a rising flood of eloquence.

But that fine capacity for forming and maintaining a 'relation' worked, inevitably, within definite limits. He was obliged to create impassa-
ble barriers between himself and the rest of mankind before he could

stretch out his eager hands over safe walls to beckon and to bless. He loved his friends, but he was condemned by the law of his being to keep clear of any really entangling net of human affection and exaction. His contacts had to be subordinate, or indeed ancillary, to the vocation he had followed with a single passion from the time when, as a small boy, he obtained a report from his tutor as showing no great aptitude for anything but a felicitous rendering of La Fontaine's fables into English. Nothing could be allowed to interfere for long with the labour from which Henry James never rested, unless perhaps during sleep. When his 'morning stint of inventive work' was over, he went forth to the renewed assault of the impressions that were always lying in wait for him. He was perpetually and mercilessly exposed, incessantly occupied with the task of assimilating his experience, freeing the pure workable metal from the base, remoulding it into new beauty with the aid of every device of his craft. He used his friends not, as some incompletely inspired artists do, as in themselves the material of his art, but as the sources of his material. He took everything they could give and he gave it back in his books. With this constant preoccupation, it was natural that the people least interesting to him were the comparatively dumb. To be 'inarticulate' was for him the cardinal social sin. It amounted to a wilful withholding of treasures of alien experience. And if he could extract no satisfaction from contemplating the keepers of golden silence, he could gain little more from intercourse with the numerous persons he dismissed from his attention as 'simple organisms'. These he held to be mere waste of any writer's time, and it was characteristic that his constant appreciation of the works of Mrs Wharton was baffled by the popularity of *Ethan Frome*,[4] because he considered that the gifted author had spent her labour on creatures too easily comprehensible to be worth her pains. He greatly preferred *The Reef*,[5] where, as he said, 'she deals with persons really fine and complicated'.

We might arrive at the same conclusion from a study of the prefaces to the New York Edition. More often than not, the initial idea for a tale came to Henry James through the medium of other people's talk. From a welter of anecdote he could unerringly pick out the living nucleus for a reconstructed and balanced work of art. His instinct for selection was admirable, and he could afford to let it range freely among a profusion of proffered subjects, secure that it would alight on the most promising. But he liked to have the subjects presented with a little artful discrimination, even in the first instance. He was dependent on conversation, but it must be educated and up to a point intelligent conversation. There is an early letter written from Italy in 1874, in which he complains of having hardly spoken to an Italian creature in nearly a year's sojourn, 'save washerwomen and waiters. . .'.

Other wanderers might have found more of Italy in washerwomen and waiters, here guaranteed to be the true native article, than in all the nobility of Rome or the Anglo-Americans of Venice, but that was not Henry James's way. For him neither pearls nor diamonds fell from the lips of waiters and washerwomen, and princesses never walked in his world disguised as goosegirls.

Friendships are maintained by the communication of speech and letters. Henry James was a voluminous letter-writer and exhaustively communicative in his talk upon every subject but one, his own work, which was his own real life. It was not because he was indifferent to what people thought of his books that he evaded discussion about them. He was always touched and pleased by any evidence that he had been intelligently read, but he never went a step out of his way to seek this assurance. He found it safest to assume that nobody read him, and he liked his friends none the worse for their incapacity.

NOTES

Theodora Bosanquet started work as James's secretary on 10 October 1907, at which time he was engaged on the preface to *The Tragic Muse*, and continued to serve in that capacity until his death. He had interviewed her for the position at Miss Petheridge's secretarial agency in Conduit Street. Miss Bosanquet had been educated at Cheltenham Ladies' College and University College, London, and was at that time in her early twenties. In a letter to his brother William, James describes her as 'a new excellent amanuensis, a young boyish Miss Bosanquet'. She later became literary editor of *Time and Tide*, and published books of her own. Her article 'As I Remember Henry James' was published in *Time and Tide* on 3 and 10 July 1954. The article repeats some of the material in *Henry James at Work*, but also adds that James 'liked a long, undisturbed morning for work. The afternoons were given to exercise and conversation, a leisurely walk with a congenial companion.'

Theodora Bosanquet's diaries, now in the Houghton Library at Harvard, contain numerous references to James. Her diary entry relating to the interview at which she was engaged includes the following passage:

He is like Coleridge – in figure – one feels that he ought to be wearing a flowered waistcoat – very expansive – 'unrestrained' – in the lower part. He wore green trousers and a blue waistcoat with a yellow sort of check on it and a black coat – that was rather a shock. I'd imagined him as always very correctly dressed – in London. He is bald except for tufts of not very grey hair at the sides. His eyes, grey I think, are exactly what I should expect – but the rest of his face is too fat. He talks slowly but continuously – I found it hard to get in any words of my own. But he is *most* kind and considerate.

She adds that he was 'so absolutely unassuming' (quoted in *Master*, p. 368).

   1. James's last play, written in the latter part of 1909; plans for its production were abandoned, and James turned it into a novel, published in 1911. It was not staged until after his death.

   2. Published in 1910; the volume contains five stories.

   3. Published in *Harper's Magazine* in October 1909. (Miss Bosanquet is in error in describing it as appearing in 'two sections'.)

   4. Published in 1911.

   5. Published in 1912.

James Orders Marmalade*

COMPTON MACKENZIE

... it was not until the late summer of 1914 that I saw Henry James for the first time since 1891.[1] He had forgotten the visit to De Vere Gardens, but remembered what I had quite forgotten and that was his presiding at a birthday party of mine and blessing a book which one of the ladies of the company had presented to me.

Henry James had just laid on me what in a previous letter he had called 'an earnest and communicative hand' in order to 'hypnotise or otherwise bedevil' me into proceeding on the right lines for my future as a writer, when his housekeeper came in to ask if he had written to the Army and Navy Stores about the marmalade. Henry James was like a porpoise arrested in mid-leap and prevented by some mischievous sea-god from plunging back to gambol in its element.

'The marmalade, Mrs X?' he repeated.

'Because if you haven't, Mr James,' the inexorable woman continued, 'it would be as well if you wrote the order for six pots now and I'll give it to the man, who is waiting.'

James looked toward the Thames as if he contemplated a plunge through the window of 21 Carlyle Mansions to escape from this domestic exigency. Then he turned to me. 'Will you forgive me, my dear boy, if I interrupt this so absorbing ... this so delightful colloquy the pleasure of which has ...'

'Mr James, please, the man is waiting.'

'Yes, yes, Mrs X.' Then he was brooding over me again. 'Now can

* 'Henry James', *Life and Letters Today*, XXXIX (December 1943) pp. 151–5.

you, do you think, engage your attention for a few minutes while I attempt to confront this hideous problem which has ...'

'Mr James, please!'

And this time the housekeeper tapped her foot with a hint of impatience.

'In one moment, Mrs X.' He turned back to me in anxious hospitality and then picked up a volume from the table.

'Here is kind Arnold Bennett's last book. I have not yet had the time to savour it myself, but you may find ... or here is dear H. G. Wells. He is always at once so ... so ...' He clutched at the air for what H. G. Wells was.

'Mr James! Mr James! Please! This marmalade,' Mrs X interjected sharply, squashing the uncaught epithet like a clothes-moth.

Henry James made an ample gesture of despair over his thwarted solicitude for a guest's entertainment. Then unlading words from the rich cargo of his mind to pack into his theme, he began to discourse of the intrusion of the world upon the holy fane of art. I listened, with half an eye on Mrs X who I feared would presently nip the Master's ear between an exasperated finger and thumb and lead him like a schoolboy to his desk.

'The man is waiting for the order, Mr James. You were going to order six 2 lb pots of marmalade.'

Henry James extricated himself from his discourse and sat down at the desk. He raised his pen, looked round over a reproachful shoulder at the housekeeper, and in the hollow voice of a ghost, 'Marmalade?' he asked.

'Marmalade', she replied firmly. 'Six 2 lb pots of the marmalade we always have.'

Henry James poised his pen above the notepaper. He was obviously searching for the phrase which would express at once with the utmost accuracy and beauty the demand he was making upon the Army and Navy Stores. It evaded him. He turned round to me.

'I hope you are continuing to beguile this unavoidable but not therefore less deplorable ...' the left arm was raised and the hand plucking at the air was seeking a word more richly equipped than 'interruption'; but it evaded him, and he had to make the best of 'interruption' by stressing 'rup' at the expense of the other syllables, with a glance of stern reproach at Mrs X. She was unimpressed.

'Six 2 lb pots of the marmalade we always have', she repeated coldly.

Henry James bent over the desk and wrote fast. Then he thrust the missive into the hands of his housekeeper, and sighed forth as she retired an elaborate polyepithetic lament for these monstrous co-operative stores which our Frankenstein of a civilisation had created to destroy the amenity of existence.

I hesitate.to set down on paper *obiter dicta* of all but thirty years ago, because to those who never heard Henry James speak the experience is incommunicable, and if I yield to temptation and record one or two it must be without any attempt to involve myself in what would at best be mere parody.

Speaking of my novel *Carnival,* James said that the chief character by the limitation of her life as a ballet-girl was not capable of sustaining so large a story. He added quickly that he should say as much of *Madame Bovary.* Presently I was telling him that it was my intention to rewrite *Carnival* and get rid of what I now thought were mistakes of treatment. The massive face of Henry James looked what must be called horror-stricken. He laid a deterrent hand upon my shoulder and bade me banish for ever from my fancy a project so . . . would that I could recall the very adjective he at last conjured from the air, an adjective so decisive in its condemnation.

'I wasted months of labour upon the thankless, the sterile, the preposterous, the monstrous task of revision. There is not an hour of such labour that I have not regretted since. You have been granted the most precious gift that can be granted to a young writer – the ability to toss up a ball against the wall of life and catch it securely at the first rebound. You have that ability to an altogether unusual extent. None of your contemporaries, so far as I have knowledge of their work, enjoys such an immediate and direct impact, and of those in the generation before you only H. G. Wells. It is a wonderful gift but it is a dangerous gift, and I entreat you, my dear boy, to beware of that immediate and direct return of the ball into your hands, while at the same time you rejoice in it. I, on the contrary, am compelled to toss the ball so that it travels from wall to wall . . .' here with a gesture he seemed to indicate that he was standing in a titanic fives-court, following with anxious eyes the ball he had just tossed against the wall of life . . . 'from wall to wall until at last, losing momentum with every new angle from which it rebounds, the ball returns to earth and dribbles slowly to my feet when I arduously bend over, all my bones creaking, and with infinite difficulty manage to reach it and pick it up.'

On another occasion we were talking about his *Notes on Novelists*[2] and I ventured to say that some of the confidence he had inspired in me by the attention he had accorded to my work had been shaken by what seemed the equal approval he had accorded to a contemporary, Y.Z.

Again that horror-stricken expression pervaded the massive face, and the arms were raised in astonishment.

'You alarm me ... you startle ... you ... all that I supposed I had indicated, however kindly, for kindness was imperative – yet, as I perhaps all too rashly supposed, with firmness and with the sharpest and most unmistakable clarity, was that so far our excellent, our greatly loved, our dear young friend Y. had written precisely nothing.'

NOTES

On Compton Mackenzie, see p. 12.

  1. For an account of this earlier meeting, see pp. 10–12.

  2. The reference is to James's essay 'The New Novel', included in *Notes on Novelists* (1914) and originally published in the *Times Literary Supplement* (19 March and 2 April 1914) under the title 'The Younger Generation'.

Part V

Conversation

'a great and talkative man'   (W. H. Auden)

'Wholly Individual'*

E. F. BENSON

But whether or not in the early days his speech had a directness corresponding to his work, I cannot imagine anything more fascinating or more wholly individual than the manner of his talk in the later days, which certainly had much in common with the processes though not the finished product of his later style. Nothing would be further from the truth than to say that he talked like a book, but most emphatically he talked like a book of his own in the making, just as he used to dictate it, with endless erasures of speech, till he got the exact and final form of his sentences. Just so in his talk he tried word after word to express the precise shade he required; he avoided, just as he avoided in his writing, any definite and final statement, if what he meant to say could be conveyed in a picturesque and allusive periphrasis. The most trivial incident thus became something rich and sumptuous with the hints of this cumulative treatment. I remember, as the simplest instance, how he described a call he paid at dusk on some neighbours at Rye, how he rang the bell and nothing happened, how he rang again and again, waited, how at the end there came steps in the passage and the door was slowly opened, and there appeared in advance on the threshold, 'something black, something canine'.[1] To have said a black dog, would not have done at all: he eschewed all such bald statements in these entrancing narrations, during which he involved himself in enormous and complicated sentences, all rolling and sonorous to the ear, as if he was composing aloud.

I was staying with him once at Lamb House in Rye in the quite early days of his ownership; a book of his was in progress, so every morning after breakfast he sequestered himself in the garden-room, and till lunch time perambulated between window and fireplace, dictating it to his typist in an intermittent rumble. Hour after hour on those hot June mornings, as one sat in the garden outside, the sound of his voice as he

* *As We Were* (London: Longmans, 1930) pp. 279–81.

composed, punctuated by the clack of the typewriter came rolling out through the tassels of wistaria which overhung the open window. Then came a morning when he emerged some half hour before his ususal time, and he took me by the arm and walked me up and down the lawn.

'An event has occurred today,' he said, exactly as if he was still dictating, 'which no doubt to you, fresh from your loud, your reverberating London, with its mosaic of multifarious movements and intensive interests, might seem justly and reasonably enough to be scarcely perceptible in all that hum and hurry and hubbub, but to me here in little Rye, tranquil and isolated little Rye, a silted up Cinque-port but now far from the sea and more readily accessible to bicyclists and pedestrians than to sea captains and smugglers; Rye, where, at the present moment, so happily, so blessedly I hold you trapped in my little corner, my angulus terrae—' On and on went the rich interminable sentence, shaped and modelled under his handling and piled with picturesque phrases which I can no longer recapture; and then I suppose (not having a typist to read it over to him) he despaired of ever struggling free of the python-coils of subordinate clauses and allusive parentheses, for he broke off short and said, 'In point of fact, my dear Fred Benson, I have finished my book.' It took a long time to arrive at that succinct statement, but the progress towards it, though abandoned, was like some adventure in a gorgeous jungle, a tropical forest of interlaced verbiage. All other talk, when he was of the company, seemed thin and jejune by this elaborate discourse, to which one listened entranced by its humours and its decorations.

I must tell too, not only for the sake of his decorative speech, but on account of the catastrophic sequel in which I was miserably involved, the story of the two nimble and fashionable dames who had a thirst for the capture of celebrities. Both longed to add Henry James to their collections, and having ascertained that he was at Rye, they travelled down from London, rang the bell at Lamb House, and sent in their cards. He did not much relish these ruthless methods but, after all, they were in earnest, for they had come far in pursuit, and with much courtesy he showed them his house, refreshed them with tea, and took them for a stroll through the picturesque little town, guiding them to the church and the gun-garden, and the Ypres tower and the Elizabethan inn. The appearance of these two brilliant strangers in his company naturally aroused a deal of pleasant interest among his friends in Rye, and next day one of them called on him, bursting with laudable curiosity to know who these dazzling creatures were. She made an arch and pointed allusion to the two pretty ladies with whom she had seen him yesterday.

'Yes,' he said, 'I believe, indeed I noticed, that there were some faint traces of bygone beauty on the face of one of the two poor wantons. . .'

NOTE

On E. F. Benson, see p. 73.
1. For a slightly different version of this anecdote, see p. 90.

'Always the Lion'*

C. LEWIS HIND

[Henry Harland][1] lived in a flat in the Cromwell Road, and there on Saturday evenings, in the big room, he liked to entertain his staff and friends. Henry James had a way of dropping in, 'Just for the space of one moment or so, my dear Harland, for I am mortally unwell tonight'. James was always the lion. Massive and bland, he would sit surrounded by his admirers, affecting to be upset by Harland's wild rushes from one guest to another, talking to each rapidly, huskily and intermittently drinking gallons of milk. . . .

It was Ford Madox Hueffer[2] who introduced me to Henry James when we were living at Winchelsea. He walked me over to Lamb House, Rye, where Henry James lived. I see this great American now, reclining on summer afternoons in a low chair in his walled garden, reading the latest French novel; or one would *hear* him dictating to his typewriter operator, who was placed behind a screen. 'I conceal her, my dear friend, as a protection against – er – a possible temperament.'

When I knew Henry James better – and to know him was to love him – I asked permission to bring two ladies to tea. The conversation flagged; we were all a little shy. To ease the strain, I praised his canary. Whereupon Henry James unclouded his dome brow and said, 'Yes, yes, the little creature sings his song of adoration each morning with – er – the slightest modicum of encouragement from me.'

* *Naphtali* (London: John Lane, 1926) pp. 89–92.

A few months later a friend said to me, 'I've been staying with Henry James. Your name cropped up.' He said, 'Lewis Hind – oh, yes – he brought two females to see me last summer'; then, reflectively, 'One of the wantons had a certain languorous grace.'

I liked to put posers to this ripe and delightful man, because he would bring his intellect to bear solemnly upon anything. A weekly journal called *The Pelican* had instituted a competition to decide, by the votes of its readers, which was the most attractive burlesque actress. I bought the issue containing a page of the prize beauties, purposing to enjoy them pictorially in the train going to Winchelsea. Henry James was in the carriage. After a few remarks about the weather, I handed him *The Pelican*, saying, 'What do you think of these, sir?'

He examined each prize beauty, carefully, then folded the paper and handed it back to me, saying, 'My dear friend, life is so crowded with various and conflicting interests that I am obliged rigorously to curtail my field of vision.'

NOTES

Charles Lewis Hind (1862–1927), journalist, author and art historian, edited *The Academy* from 1896 to 1903.

1. Henry Harland (1861–1905), American author, settled in London and was a great admirer of James. Harland became editor of *The Yellow Book* in 1894 and published James's story 'The Death of the Lion' in the first number. It was Harland who introduced Aubrey Beardsley to James.

2. See p. 21.

'An Extraordinary Candour'*

ELIZABETH JORDAN

At times he also talked with an extraordinary candour. Once he told me of a young disciple of his who insisted on sitting at his feet – where, I inferred, he was very much in his great master's way. Mr James grew so

* *Three Rousing Cheers*, pp. 211–12.

weary of having him there that he pulled wires and found an opening for the youth in Canada – a country far removed from Mr James's feet.

'I went to see him off', Mr James ended exuberantly. 'I was afraid he would discover how delighted I was to see him off. I shook hands with him again and again. Then, at the last moment, just as the train was leaving the station, I emptied all my pockets and gave him every penny I had with me.'

Mr James stopped and looked at me with the wide grin of an impish little boy. 'I had taken pains not to have too much money with me!' he ended.

Another time he described to me his sole meeting with Thackeray, when the latter was making his first visit to America. Mr James was an infant of six at the time, clad in a new suit decorated with shining brass buttons.

'They covered me as stars cover the sky', Mr James said. 'I was dazzled by them. I expected Mr Thackeray to be dazzled, too. But my buttons amused him, and he laughed. It was a terrible experience for me. I have never forgotten it – for in that moment I experienced my first sense of disillusionment.'

NOTE

On Elizabeth Jordan, see p. 45.

James on Intolerance*

RAYMOND BLATHWAYT

Many years ago Herbert Tree[1] and I went down together to spend a night in the wonderful old city of Rye. After breakfast on the following morning we paid a call on Henry James, who was then living in Rye. Tree and he did most of the talking, which turned upon the topic of intolerance. Tree, by way of illustration, told James of an incident which

* *Looking Down the Years* (London: Allen & Unwin, 1935) pp. 288–9.

had happened to himself, when a clergyman had attacked him, very fiercely, and also very unjustly, for holding up the clerical profession to ridicule in his dramatised version of *Trilby*,[2] which contained a very slight and very innocent presentation of a Church of England clergyman, admirably played by Will Haviland.[3] James shook his enormous head gravely and sadly as he replied: 'Intolerance is of the devil, and yet, contradictorily enough, it often appears to me to be the outstanding characteristic of the Church and the priestly mind. Let me give you an instance of it.' And he proceeded to read the following: 'It is better for sun and moon to drop from heaven, for the earth to fail, and for all the many millions in it to die of starvation in extremest agony, as far as temporal affliction goes, than that one soul, I will not say should be lost, but should commit one venal sin, should tell one wilful untruth, or should steal one poor farthing without excuse.'

'I did not think it could have been possible,' he continued, 'to produce such an incredible instance of exaggeration as is contained in this almost insane sentence pronounced by John Henry Newman.'[4]

A famous bishop once preached a sermon upon the exceeding sinfulness of little sins, but even he could not have imagined such a ridiculously perverted conception of what a little innocent wrong can be twisted and tortured into by the diseased and fevered imagination of an ill-regulated and wholly uncontrolled religious fanatic. And yet it was John Henry Newman who also wrote so touchingly of those 'angel faces which we have loved long since and lost awhile!'[5]

'I would like,' continued Mr James, to 'make a really scientific study of the whole history of religious intolerance, which is, I really believe, the history of humanity.'

NOTES

Raymond Blathwayt (1855–1935) was an author and journalist.

1. Sir Herbert Beerbohm Tree (1853–1917), celebrated actor–manager.

2. George Du Maurier's popular novel *Trilby* (1894) had been adapted for the stage by the American dramatist Paul Potter and produced in the United States in 1895. Beerbohm Tree produced it in England and played Svengali; it opened at the Haymarket Theatre on 30 October 1895 and was a huge success. In a letter written in August 1895 to Du Maurier, who was suffering from pre-production anxieties, James said that 'my sympathetic bosom expands to you'.

3. English actor.

4. J. H. Newman (1801–90) was for many years a leading figure in nineteenth-century religious and sectarian controversy. The quotation is from his *Lectures on Anglican Difficulties*, Lecture 8 (1850).

5. Adapted from Newman's famous hymn 'Lead, Kindly Light', written in 1833.

James Asks the Way*

EDITH WHARTON

Not infrequently, on my annual visit to Qu'acre,[1] I 'took off' from Lamb House, where I also went annually for a visit to Henry James. The motor run between Rye and Windsor being an easy one, I was often accompanied by Henry James, who generally arranged to have his visit to Qu'acre coincide with mine. James, who was a frequent companion on our English motor-trips, was firmly convinced that, because he lived in England, and our chauffeur (an American) did not, it was necessary that the latter should be guided by him through the intricacies of the English countryside. Signposts were rare in England in those days, and for many years afterward, and a truly British reserve seemed to make the local authorities reluctant to communicate with the invading stranger. Indeed, considerable difficulty existed as to the formulating of advice and instructions, and I remember in one village the agitated warning: 'Motorists! Beware of the children!' – while in general there was a marked absence of indications as to the whereabouts of the next village.

It chanced, however, that Charles Cook, our faithful and skilful driver, was a born path-finder, while James's sense of direction was non-existent, or rather actively but always erroneously alert; and the consequences of his intervention were always bewildering, and sometimes extremely fatiguing. The first time that my husband and I went to Lamb House by motor (coming from France) James, who had travelled to Folkestone by train to meet us, insisted on seating himself next to Cook, on the plea that the roads across Romney marsh formed such a tangle that only an old inhabitant could guide us to Rye. The suggestion resulted in our turning around and around in our tracks till long after dark, though Rye, conspicuous on its conical hill, was just ahead of us, and Cook could easily have landed us there in time for tea.

Another year we had been motoring in the west country, and on the way back were to spend a night at Malvern. As we approached (at the close of a dark rainy afternoon) I saw James growing restless, and was

* *A Backward Glance*, pp. 239–43.

not surprised to hear him say: 'My dear, I once spent a summer at Malvern, and know it very well; and as it is rather difficult to find the way to the hotel, it might be well if Edward were to change places with me, and let me sit beside Cook.' My husband of course acceded(though with doubt in his heart), and James having taken his place, we awaited the result. Malvern, if I am not mistaken, is encircled by a sort of upper boulevard, of the kind called in Italy a *strada di circonvallazione*, and for an hour we circled about above the outspread city, while James vainly tried to remember which particular street led down most directly to our hotel. At each corner (literally) he stopped the motor, and we heard a muttering, first confident and then anguished. 'This – this, my dear Cook, yes ... this certainly is the right corner. But no; stay! A moment longer, please – in this light it's so difficult ... appearances are so misleading ... It may be ... yes! I think it *is* the next turn ... "a little farther lend thy guiding hand" ... that is, drive on; but slowly, please, my dear Cook; *very* slowly!' And at the next corner the same agitated monologue would be repeated; till at length Cook, the mildest of men, interrupted gently: 'I guess any turn'll get us down into the town, Mr James, and after that I can ask. –' and late, hungry and exhausted we arrived at length at our destination, James still convinced that the next turn would have been the right one, if only we had been more patient.

The most absurd of these episodes occurred on another rainy evening, when James and I chanced to arrive at Windsor long after dark. We must have been driven by a strange chauffeur – perhaps Cook was on a holiday; at any rate, having fallen into the lazy habit of trusting to him to know the way, I found myself at a loss to direct his substitute to the King's Road. While I was hesitating, and peering out into the darkness, James spied an ancient doddering man who had stopped in the rain to gaze at us. 'Wait a moment, my dear – I'll ask him where we are'; and leaning out he signalled to the spectator.

'My good man, if you'll be good enough to come here, please; a little nearer – so', and as the old man came up: 'My friend, to put it to you in two words, this lady and I have just arrived here from *Slough*; that is to say, to be more strictly accurate, we have recently *passed through* Slough on our way here, having actually motored to Windsor from Rye, which was our point of departure; and the darkness having overtaken us, we should be much obliged if you would tell us where we now are in relation, say, to the High Street, which, as you of course know, leads to the Castle, after leaving on the left hand the turn down to the railway station.'

I was not surprised to have this extraordinary appeal met by silence, and a dazed expression on the old wrinkled face at the window; nor to have James go on: 'In short' (his invariable prelude to a fresh series of explanatory ramifications), 'in short, my good man, what I want to put to you in a word is this: supposing we have already (as I have reason to think we have) driven past the turn down to the railway station (which, in that case, by the way, would probably not have been on our left hand, but on our right), where are we now in relation to . . .'

'Oh, please,' I interrupted, feeling myself utterly unable to sit through another parenthesis, 'do ask him where the King's Road is.'

'Ah – ? The King's Road? Just so! Quite right! Can you, as a matter of fact, my good man, tell us where, in relation to our present position, the King's Road exactly *is*?'

'Ye're in it', said the aged face at the window.

NOTE

On Edith Wharton, see p. 27.
  1. Queen's Acre, Howard Sturgis's home at Windsor.

Talking like a Book*

G. W. E. RUSSELL

If there ever was a man who talked like a book – and one of his own books too – that man is Mr Henry James. With grave aspect and in a darkling undertone, he pronounces his solemn gnomes and mysterious epigrams, or propounds those social and psychical conundrums which supply his devout admirers the largest part of their intellectual exercise. But, as Sir George Trevelyan judiciously observes,

> The gravest of us now and then unbends,
> And likes his glass of claret and his friends.[1]

And when this softening change has passed over Mr James he becomes a delightful companion. He has the desirable qualities of fine appreciation

* 'Talk and Talkers of To-day', *New Review*, I (August 1889) p. 241.

and genuine sympathy; he observes closely and remarks justly; talks, not much indeed, but always with tact and discrimination; is always ready to please and be pleased; and, without being in the slightest degree a flatterer or a parasite, enjoys the happy knack of putting those to whom he speaks in good conceit with themselves.

NOTE

George William Erskine Russell (1853–1919), English journalist.

1. Quoted from Sir George Otto Trevelyan's Cambridge squib 'Horace at the University of Athens', included in *The Ladies in Parliament and Other Pieces* (Cambridge: Deighton, Bell, 1869).

Meetings with James (1901–15)*

A. C. BENSON

(a) [January 1901] He talked interestingly but pessimistically of every-body. There are no writers, it would seem, and no readers.... I asked him about Mrs H[umphry] Ward's books,[1] and he said that they were not books at all to him – *characters*, conscientious information, but no *situations*. (This of *Eleanor*.) It seems Mrs Ward sends him her books for criticism, 'but I have to write dilatory and perfunctory letters – in fact, my dear Arthur, the only language which Mrs Ward comprehends is the language of *adulation*'. He was very affectionate and nice.

(b) [Early 1902] He was delightful, though suffering from gout.... He talked very freely and with a good deal of gesture and solemnity. He said

* (e), (g), (h) and (j) are taken from *The Diary of Arthur Christopher Benson*, ed. Percy Lubbock (New York: Longmans, Green, 1926) pp. 81–2, 225–6, 273, 280–1. The other extracts are taken from Benson's manuscript diary at Magdalene College, Cambridge, and are printed here by kind permission of the Master and Fellows of Magdalene College.

that having once learnt to *dictate* he could never do anything else. *To walk about!* that was the secret. The old cramped position, the weary hand – 'My dear Arthur, it's shame, it's ruin, it's horror unutterable!' But I think his work has got hold of him too much, and is now too integral a part of his life.... I still regret the beard; he looks to me dumpy and undignified without it; but what a tender and loyal heart!

(c) [1903] H[enry] James looked *remarkably* well – a good colour; and generally tranquil – none of the alabastrine, dark-eyed, knitted look he sometimes wears – but a kind of dumpy *bonhomme*.

(d) [March 1904; Benson dined at Edmund Gosse's, where James and H. G. Wells were among the guests. After dinner James] inveighed against the century as the most shameless and hypocritical that had ever dawned. He seized Lady Jekyll's[2] arm, after poking at it with a little finger, and held it, gently shaking it – 'My dear lady, the heart of the age is eaten out, is eaten out by vile newspaperism – why, in God's name, all this fuss, all this screaming? Why is there no *peace*?'

(e) [29 April 1904; into the smoking-room of the Athenaeum Club] there entered Henry James, Thomas Hardy and another, an owlish man, lantern-jawed and bald, with a mildness of demeanour which I disliked, but which I am conscious that I am apt to assume, when shy.

I took H. J. to a secluded seat, and we had a talk. ... I questioned him about his ways of work. He admitted that he worked *every* day, dictated every morning, and began a new book the instant the old one was finished. He said it was his only chance because he worked so slowly, and excised so much. I asked him when the inception and design of a *new* book was formed; and he gave no satisfactory answer to this except to roll his eyes, to wave his hand about, to pat my knee and to say, 'It's all *about*, it's about – it's in the air – it, so to speak, follows me and dogs me.' Then Hardy came up and sat down the other side of me. I make it a rule *never* to introduce myself to the notice of distinguished men, unless they recognise me; Hardy had looked at me, then looked away, suffused by a misty smile, and I presently gathered that this was a recognition – he seemed hurt by my not speaking to him. ... Then we had an odd triangular talk. Hardy could not hear what H. J. said, nor H. J. what Hardy said; and I had to try and keep the ball going. I felt like Alice between the two

Queens. Hardy talked rather interestingly of Newman.... We talked of Maxime Du Camp[3] and Flaubert, and H. J. delivered himself very oracularly on the latter. Then Hardy went away wearily and kindly. Then H. J. and I talked of Howard's *Belchamber*.[4] H. J. said that it was a good idea, a good situation. 'He kindly read it to me; and we approached the dénouement in a pleasant Thackerayan manner – and then it was suddenly all at an end. He had had his chance and he had made *nothing* of it. Good Heavens, I said to myself, he has made nothing of it! I tried, with a thousand subterfuges and doublings, such as one uses with the work of a friend, to indicate this. I hinted that the *interest* of the situation was not the *experiences* – which were dull and shabby and disagreeable enough in all conscience, and not disguised by the aristocratic atmosphere – not the *experiences*, but the *effect* of the fall of wave after disastrous wave upon Sainty's *soul* – if one can use the expression for such a spark of quality as was inside the poor rat – that was the interest, and I said to myself, "Good God, why this chronicle, if it is a mere passage, a mere ante-chamber, and leads to nothing." '

I think I have got this marvellous tirade nearly correct....

(f) [14 February 1906; Benson lunched with James at the Athenaeum.] H. J. eats slower than I ever saw anyone eat. He looks very well, I think – like a comfortable French priest – fatter, sleeker, browner, less heavy-eyed. He talked much of Gosse; and I never saw his gestures more eloquent. He raised his hands again and again to heaven in protest; and closed his eyes in meek acquiescence. 'Poor dear Gosse – a man with whom one becomes aware that any increase of intimate relation is an increase of personal danger, of danger – I could relate instances to you, but no matter.... His frivolity, his incurable frivolity! – his felinity, his instinctive, his deep-seated felinity! and yet the poor fellow is affectionate, caninely affectionate. He loves you, even while he defames and endangers you! I am sure of that' – and so on with quick glances at me – it was incomparably amusing and all too short. He promised to come to Cambridge 'so long as I may linger and loiter, in my own hopelessly futile way, at an *inn*!'

(g) [8 November 1911] Went to Athenaeum. Then Henry James appeared, looking stout and well, and rather excitedly cheerful. He would not talk, but hurried off to order his dinner. I had induced him not to attend the lecture – it would be farcical impudence for me to hold forth to him! He returned at 7.30, and we sat down together. There is something about him which was not there before, something stony, strained, anxious. But he was deeply affectionate and talked very characteristically. He said of P.'s article on William Morris that it was charming, but began at the wrong end – that it was a well-combed, well-dressed figure, and that P. had overlooked the bloody, lusty, noisy *grotesque* elements in Morris. 'In these things, my dear Arthur, we must always be *bloody*.' . . . He had read Arnold Bennett. 'The fact is that I am so *saturated* with impressions that I can't take in new ones. I have lived my life, I have worked out my little conceptions, I have an idea how it all ought to be done – and here comes a man with his great voluminous books, dripping with detail – but with no scheme, no conception of character, no *subject* – perhaps a vague idea of just sketching a character or two – and then comes this great panorama, everything perceived, nothing seen *into*, nothing related. He's not afraid of masses and crowds and figures – but one asks oneself what is it all for, where does it all tend, what's the *aim* of it?'

By this time we had dawdled and pecked our way through our dinner – he ate a hearty meal, and there was much of that delicious gesture, the upturned eye, the clenched upheld hand, and that jolly laughter that begins in the middle of a sentence and permeates it all. . . .

Then he spoke about Hugh Walpole – he said he was charming in his zest for experience and his love of intimacies. 'I often think,' he went on, 'if I look back at my own starved past, that I wish I had done more, reached out further, claimed more – and I should be the last to block the way. The only thing is to be there, to wait, to sympathise, to help if necessary.' . . . He joined all this with many pats and caressing gestures; then led me down by the arm and sent me off with a blessing. I felt he was glad that I should go – had felt the strain – but that he was well and happy. He is a wonderful person, so entirely simple in emotion and loyalty, so complicated in mind. His little round head, his fine gestures, even to the waiters – 'I am not taking any of this – I don't need this' – his rolling eyes, with the heavy lines round them, his rolling resolute gait, as if he *shouldered* something and set off with his burden – all very impressive.[5]

(h) [18 April 1914] Back to the Athenaeum, and fell in with Henry James, very portly and gracious – a real delight. I had tea with him, and he talked very richly. . . . He complimented me grotesquely and effusively as likely to incur the jealousy of the gods for my success and efficiency.

He little knows! My books are derided, my activities are small and fussy. I said this, and he smiled benignantly.

I asked him if he was well. He said solemnly that he lived (touching his heart) with a troublesome companion, angina pectoris. 'But you look well.' He laughed – 'I *look*, my dear Arthur, I admit I *look* – but at that point I can accompany you no further. It's a look, I allow.' And so we said good-bye; he shook my hands often very affectionately. I have a feeling that I shall not see him again.

(i) [12 April 1915] He said I looked adventurous so I told him of my defying my lawyer. He said, 'I can't, my dear Arthur, without further comment and enquiry do full justice to your anecdote. But I will take it away and reflect on it – and you may depend upon my extracting from it something to your advantage.' He looked worn and small but sturdy and gave me a blessing.

(j) [21 April 1915] I lunched with Henry James, who kept on being entangled by voluble persons. . . . H. J. was very tremendous; he looks ill, he changes colour, he is dark under the eyes – but he was in a cheerful and pontifical mood. He ate a plentiful meal of veal and pudding, but he spoke to me very gravely of his physical condition and his chronic angina . . . We went down together, and he made me a most affectionate farewell. He is slower and more *soigneux* in utterance than ever, but leaves a deep impression of majesty, beauty and greatness. He said that his life was now one flurried escape from sociability, but he valued a glimpse of me.

(k) [July 1915] I went up to speak to him, and asked for his blessing. H. J. caught my arm and said, 'My dear Arthur, my blessing is always so ardently and intently yours, and so continuously broods over you, that if you ask me to extend it to you, I must begin by withholding it' – he gave a bubbling laugh.

NOTES

On A. C. Benson, see p. 89. Benson noted on 3 October 1897 that he had lent his diary to James, who in a letter had described it as 'a series of data on the life of a young Englishman of great endowments, character and position at the end of the nineteenth century'. Benson commented: 'I don't know anyone like H. J. for throwing a halo, restoring one's sense of dignity, and I value this.'

1. See p. 42.
2. Lady Agnes Jekyll (1861–1937), wife of Col. Sir Herbert Jekyll.
3. Maxime Du Camp (1822–94), French poet and novelist.
4. Novel (1904) by Howard Sturgis (1855–1920).
5. Among the passages omitted from this entry in the version printed by Percy Lubbock is the following reference to H. G. Wells: 'He talked of Wells with much interest – said he had not improved, that he was always saying (this was apropos of Wells's article about the novel in the *Fortnightly*) what "we" were going to do. "Good God, what a waste of time! Go and *do* it, my dear man, get it *done!*"'

'A Kind of Mutual Agony'*

MURIEL DRAPER

At Mrs Napier's house one day I met Henry James. . . . He stood, a solid squared ashlar of wisdom, with a magnificently domed head atop, in Mrs Napier's drawing-room. I walked up to him as bravely as I could, and we met. I told him how it had come about that he had entered my childhood as a uniquely living genius. He listened, with a burdened smile on his full lips, he who had to hear so much, and then it began. With a labouring that began stirring in the soles of his feet and worked up with Gargantuan travail through his knees and weighty abdomen to his heaving breast and strangled column of a throat, hoisted up by eyebrows raised high over the most steadily watching eyes I have ever looked into, he spoke. Having imaginatively participated in every effort his body had made, I was exhausted by the time the words were finally born, but had awaited them too long not to rally my attention when I heard them. They were about like this:

'My dear, – if I may call you so, my dear, – my even now – if I may yet further without permission so invade your, to be sure, passing years – child, my dear child. How right and yet how perfectly – if perfection can so enter, how perfectly wrong they both were, *you* were, all of you were.'

I sat down. He sat beside me, and in a kind of mutual agony, we

Music at Midnight (London: Heinemann, 1929) pp. 86, 87–92.

continued. I was later to discover that there was a way of communication with him that avoided all this amazing difficulty, which allowed the rich vein of his knowledge of human beings and events to flow unchecked, and which made listening to him and talking with him one of the rare values of my life, but this first time was agony. Again and again, in that memorable conversation, he would raise those cornices of eyebrows in an effort to build under them the astounding structure of words that so decorate his written page, and again and again would fail to find them. He seemed to listen for them with his own ear as eagerly as I with mine and even kept his eye alert for the possible shape of one that might appear by happy accident. Rejecting any less felicitous expression of his thought than one that would perfectly convey it, he would throw one phrase after the other away on its tremendous journey up from the soles of his feet. A patient 'er – er – er' was the only sign that another had fallen by the wayside. Once, with temerity, I offered him one, almost beseeching him to take it as agreed counterfeit until such time as real gold would be passed over the counter and this soul-racking barter cease. But no, with the dear heavy smile leaving his lips to rest for a moment somewhere under his eyes, he cast it aside. So it went. The weight of his thought, the penetrating justice of his wit, and the impact of his whole being were such that I would gladly have suffered the pain of its articulation through years of silence, had they not seemed to me also 'to be sure, passing years'.

We spoke of America a little tentatively, a little anxiously and very tenderly. We spoke of families. He heard there was a son. He wanted to know him. He spoke of Ruth Draper[1] and her talent. He spoke of music and asked to come one night to Edith Grove and listen. And then, as I pulled myself up and away from his side, fascinated, exhausted and adoring, his eyes travelled up from under the corniced eyebrows and saw my hat. It was a small white satin affair, with a cluster of tiny white love birds perched at the front. He gasped with horror, pointed his finger, and said with utter kindness, 'My child,' (it came easier this time), 'my very dear child – the cruelty – ah! the cruelty of your hat! That once living – indeed yes, loving, – creatures should have been so cruelly separated by death to become so unhappily and yet, ah! how becomingly united on your hat.'

I had met Henry James! . . .

Soon after he came to lunch. Crossing the threshold of Edith Grove, he questioned me as to the tenure of the house. How long a lease did we have? How long would we be there? I told him it was a twenty-one-year lease and he sighed ponderously, saying, 'Long enough to see me out, my child, long enough to see me out. Stay me out, I beg – stay me out.' He

had asked to be quite alone, so Paul and I sat one on either side of him
and listened. After lunch he and I went down to the studio through the
staircase where the lady harpist had remained so long imprisoned. He
asked to see my son, so that young person was sent for. The Irish angel
brought him. He was only a little over three years old, and a few days
before had been found asleep with a copy of Henry James's book, *Letters
of a Son and Brother*, under his pillow, his hand slipped in at a page upon
which a photograph of Henry and his brother William standing close to
their father's knee was reproduced. The tale of this incident had moved
Henry James and when my son came into the room he fastened his
accurately wise eye upon him. The Irish angel had brushed his hair until
it shone, and dressed him in his best afternoon raiment, which consisted
of long linen trousers and suspenders cut out of one piece, fastened to a
frilled white shirt at the shoulders by a huge pearl button. The devouring
James focused his gaze on that button and held it there as the child
crossed the vast room. Spontaneously glad to see this grown-up who in
his youth had leaned so trustingly at his father's knee, my son had
entered the room on the run, but faced with the arresting force of his
gaze, his footsteps faltered and his pace slackened, so that by the time he
came to within three feet of Henry James, he stopped short and remained
motionless as that great man began to address him:

'Ah! my boy. So here you come, faithfully – as it were, into view – with
buttons, yes, *buttons* ...' Here he paused while the yeast that would
eventually give rise to the ultimate word began to ferment in the soles of
his feet: as it reached his knees he repeated, 'Buttons, that are, er – that
are – er er ...' By this time the poor child was intimidated by the
intensity of tone and started to back away, but Henry James began a
circular movement in the air, with the forefinger of his right hand and
continued – 'buttons that have been – er,' – and then in a shout of
triumph – '*jettés-D*, as it were, yes, *jettés-d*' – his voice quieting down as
the word emerged, – '*jettés-d* so rightly, so needfully, just there, my child',
pointing in the direction of his small shoulder. But my child heard him
not. At the first burst of '*jettés-D*' he had fled terrified from the room, the
discovery of which brought forth from Henry James the mournful
reflection, 'Would I had remained a photograph!'

To be called to the telephone by Henry James was an experience in
itself. The first time it happened I, all unaware, took up the receiver
eagerly, and said, 'Yes – this is Muriel.'

A voice that began to twist and turn on the other end of the wire,
finally spoke.

'Would you be – er – or rather, my dear, – er – my very dear, if I may
call you so, child, would you, – not by – er – er *arrangement*, but would you

– more – er – truthfully speaking – be – er – er NATURALLY at home – this afternoon?'

By that time I was not naturally anything at all, and could only gasp, 'Yes, always, any time – yes, yes, this afternoon at five, I will, unnaturally or not, be here – yes', and hung up.

It was during this visit that I learned to talk with him and listen to him, by withdrawing the weight of my attention from his actual words and the anguished facial contortions that accompanied them, and fastening it on the stream of thought itself. I even diverted my eyes from that part of his face from which the phrases finally emerged, namely, his mouth, and directed them to a more peaceful spot between his eyes, which I imagined to be the source of thought. It proved helpful. Evidently released from some bondage which the eye and ear of a listener imposed upon him, he seemed to feel more free. My effort to ignore the words and extract the meaning by a sense of weight, inflection and rhythm which emanated from him, removed the burden he must have felt at keeping me – anyone – waiting so long, and gradually the full current of his thought was flowing steadily, pauses and hesitations becoming accents rather than impediments. It proved an excellent *modus operandi* from then on, and only at those times when he had an audience of more than one person did the old difficulties return.

NOTE

1. Ruth Draper (1884–1956), American actress, became famous for her monologues. James met her in 1913 and wrote then that 'Little Ruth is a dear of dears, and her talent has really an extraordinary charm' (see *Master*, pp. 491–2). He wrote a monologue for her (printed in *The Complete Plays of Henry James*) but it was never performed, since she always composed her own material.

'Magnifying the Minute'*

DESMOND MacCARTHY

In Henry James's later letters his voice is audible; nor is this surprising, for his letters were often dictated, and his conversation, in its search for the right word, its amplifications, hesitations and interpolated after-

* *Portraits I* (London: Putnam, 1931) pp. 149–55.

thoughts, resembled dictation. This sounds portentous, not to say boring; indeed, it was at times embarrassing. But – and this made all the difference – he was fascinating. The spell he exercised by his style was exercised in his conversation. Phrases of abstruse exaggerated drollery or of the last intellectual elegance flowered in it profusely. At first you might feel rather conscience-stricken for having set in motion, perhaps by a casual question, such tremendous mental machinery. It seemed really too bad to have put him to such trouble, made him work and weigh his words like that; and if, through the detestable habit of talking about anything rather than be silent, you had started a topic in which you were not interested, you might be well punished. There was something at once so painstaking, serious and majestical in the procedure of his mind that you shrank from diverting it, and thus the whole of your little precious time with him might be wasted. This often happened in my case during our fifteen years' acquaintance, and I still regret those bungled opportunities.

In conversation he could not help giving his best, the stereotyped and perfunctory being abhorrent to him. Each talk was thus a fresh adventure, an opportunity of discovering for himself what he thought about books and human beings. His respect for his subject was only equalled, one noticed, by his respect for that delicate instrument for recording and comparing impressions, his own mind. He absolutely refused to hustle it, and his conversational manner was largely composed of reassuring and soothing gestures intended to allay, or anticipate, signs of impatience. The sensation of his hand on my shoulder in our pausing rambles together was, I felt, precisely an exhortation to patience. 'Wait,' that reassuring pressure seemed to be humorously saying, 'wait. I know, my dear fellow, you are getting fidgety; but wait – and we shall enjoy together the wild pleasure of discovering what "Henry James" thinks of this matter. For my part, I dare not hurry him!' His possession of this kind of double consciousness was one of the first characteristics one noticed; and sure enough we would often seem both to be waiting, palpitating with the same curiosity, for an ultimate verdict. At such moments the working of his mind fascinated me, as though I were watching through a window some hydraulic engine, its great smooth wheel and shining piston moving with ponderous ease through a vitreous dusk. The confounding thing was that the great machine could be set in motion by a penny in the slot!

I remember the first time I met him (the occasion was an evening party) I asked him if he thought London 'beautiful' – an idiotic question; worse than that, a question to which I did not really want an answer, though there were hundreds of others (some no doubt also idiotic) which

I was longing to ask. But it worked. To my dismay it worked only too well. 'London? Beautiful?' he began, with that considering slant of his massive head I was to come to know so well, his lips a little ironically compressed, as though he wished to keep from smiling too obviously. 'No: hardly beautiful. It is too chaotic, too – ' then followed a discourse upon London and the kind of appeal it made to the historic sense, even when it starved the aesthetic, which I failed to follow; so dismayed was I at having, by my idiot's question, set his mind working at such a pitch of concentration on a topic indifferent to me. I was distracted, too, by anxiety to prove myself on the spot intelligent; and the opportunity of interjecting a comment which might conceivably attain that object seemed to grow fainter and fainter while he hummed and havered and rolled along. How should I feel afterwards if I let slip this chance, perhaps the last, of expressing my admiration and my gratitude! At the end of a sentence, the drift of which had escaped me, but which closed, I think, with the words 'find oneself craving for a whiff of London's carboniferous damp', I did however interrupt him. Enthusiasm and questions (the latter regarding *The Awkward Age*, just out) poured from my lips. A look of bewilderment, almost of shock, floated for a moment over his fine, large, watchful, shaven face, on which the lines were so lightly etched. For a second he opened his rather prominent hazel eyes a shade wider, an expansion of the eyelids that to my imagination seemed like the adjustment at me of the lens of a microscope; then the great engine was slowly reversed, and, a trifle grimly, yet ever so kindly, and with many reassuring pats upon the arm, he said: 'I understand, my dear boy, what you mean – and I thank you.' (Ouf! What a relief!)

He went on to speak of *The Awkward Age*. 'Flat' was, it appeared, too mild an expression to describe its reception, 'My books make no more sound or ripple now than if I dropped them one after the other into mud.' And he had, I learnt to my astonishment, in writing that searching diagnosis of sophisticated relations, conceived himself to be following in the footsteps, 'of course, with a difference', of the sprightly Gyp! Hastily and emphatically I assured him that where I came from, at Cambridge, his books were very far from making no ripple in people's minds. At this he showed some pleasure; but I noticed then, as often afterwards, that he was on his guard against being gratified by appreciation from any quarter. He liked it – everybody does, but he was exceedingly sceptical about its value. I doubt if he believed that anybody thoroughly under-stood what, as an artist, he was after, or how skilfully he had manipu-lated his themes; and speaking with some confidence for the majority of his enthusiastic readers at that time, I may say he was right.

He was fully aware of his idiosyncrasy in magnifying the minute. I remember a conversation in a four-wheeler ('the philosopher's preference', he called it) about the married life of the Carlyles. He had been re-reading Froude's *Life of Carlyle*,[1] and after remarking that he thought Carlyle perhaps the best of English letter-writers, he went on to commiserate Mrs Carlyle on her dull, drudging life. I protested against 'dull', and suggested she had at least acquired from her husband one source of permanent consolation and entertainment, namely the art of mountaining mole-hills. A look of droll sagacity came over his face, and turning sideways to fix me better and to make sure I grasped the implication, he said: 'Ah! but for that, where would *any of us* be?'

Once or twice I went a round of calls with him. I remember being struck on these occasions by how much woman there seemed to be in him; at least it was thus I explained the concentration of his sympathy upon social worries (the wrong people meeting each other, etc., etc.), or small misfortunes such as missing a train, and also the length of time he was able to expatiate upon them with interest. It struck me that women ran on in talk with him with a more unguarded volubility than they do with most men, as though they were sure of his complete understanding. I was amazed, too, by his standard of decent comfort; and his remark on our leaving what appeared to me a thoroughly well-appointed, prosperous house, 'Poor S., poor S. – the stamp of unmistakable povery upon everything!' has remained in my memory. I never ventured to ask him to my own house; not because I was ashamed of it, but because I did not wish to excite quite unnecessary commiseration. He would have imputed himself; there were so many little things in life he minded intensely which I did not mind at all. I do not think he could have sat without pain in a chair, the stuffing of which was visible in places. His dislike of squalor was so great that surroundings to be tolerable to him had positively to proclaim its utter impossibility. 'I can stand,' he once said to me, while we were waiting for our hostess in an exceptionally gilt and splendid drawing-room, 'a great deal of gold.' The effects of wealth upon character and behaviour attracted him as a novelist, but no array of terms can do justice to his lack of interest in the making of money. He was at home in describing elderly Americans who had acquired it by means of some invisible flair, and on whom its acquisition had left no mark beyond perhaps a light refined fatigue (his interest in wealth was therefore the reverse of Balzacian); or in portraying people who had inherited it. Evidence of ancient riches gave him far more pleasure than lavishness, and there we sympathised; but above all the signs of tradition and of loving discrimination exercised over many years in conditions of security soothed and delighted him. Lamb House, his home at Rye, was a perfect shell for his sensibility. He was in the habit of speaking of its 'inconspicuous little charm', but its charm could hardly escape anyone; so quiet, dignified and *gemütlich* it was, within, without.

But an incident comes back to me which struck me as revealing something much deeper in him than this characteristic. It occurred after a luncheon party of which he had been, as they say, 'the life'. We happened to be drinking our coffee together while the rest of the party had moved on to the verandah. 'What a charming picture they make,' he said, with his great head aslant, 'the women there with their embroidery, the ...' There was nothing in his words, anybody might have spoken them; but in his attitude, in his voice, in his whole being at that moment, I divined such complete detachment, that I was startled into speaking out of myself: 'I can't bear to look at life like that,' I blurted out, 'I want to be in everything. Perhaps that is why I cannot *write*, it makes me feel absolutely alone. ...' The effect of this confession upon him was instantaneous and surprising. He leant forward and grasped my arm excitedly: 'Yes, it is solitude. If it runs after you and catches you, well and good. But for heaven's sake don't run after *it*. It is absolute solitude.' And he got up hurriedly and joined the others. On the walk home it occurred to me that I had for a moment caught a glimpse of his intensely private life, and, rightly or wrongly, I thought that this glimpse explained much: his apprehensively tender clutch upon others, his immense pre-occupation with the surface of things and his exclusive devotion to his art. His confidence in himself in relation to that art, I thought I discerned one brilliant summer night, as we were sauntering along a dusty road which crosses the Romney marshes. He had been describing to me the spiral of depression which a recent nervous illness had compelled him step after step, night after night, day after day, to descend. He would, he thought, never have found his way up again, had it not been for a life-line thrown to him by his brother William; perhaps the only man in whom he admired equally both heart and intellect. What stages of arid rejection of life and meaningless yet frantic agitation he had been compelled to traverse! 'But,' and he suddenly stood still, 'but it has been good' – and here he took off his hat, baring his great head in the moonlight – 'for my genius.' Then, putting on his hat again, he added, 'Never cease to watch whatever happens to you.'

NOTE

Sir Desmond MacCarthy (1878–1952), critic. For an account of a visit by MacCarthy to James near the end of the latter's life (taken from an unpublished letter to Virginia Woolf), see *Master*, p. 399.

1. James Anthony Froude's biography of Carlyle (1882–4) set a new standard for biographical candour.

James Discourses 'in the Public Street'*

VIRGINIA WOOLF

... we went and had tea with Henry James today, and Mr and Mrs [George] Prothero,[1] at the golf club; and Henry James fixed me with his staring blank eye – it is like a child's marble – and said 'My dear Virginia, they tell me – they tell me – they tell me – that you – as indeed being your father's daughter nay your grandfather's grandchild – the descendant I may say of a century – of a century – of quill pens and ink – ink – ink pots, yes, yes, yes, they tell me – ahm m m – that you, that you, that you *write* in short.' This went on in the public street, while we all waited, as farmers wait for the hen to lay an egg – do they? – nervous, polite, and now on this foot now on that. I felt like a condemned person, who sees the knife drop and stick and drop again. Never did any woman hate 'writing' as much as I do. But when I am old and famous I shall discourse like Henry James. We had to stop periodically to let him shake himself free of the thing; he made phrases over the bread and butter 'rude and rapid' it was, and told us all the scandal of Rye. 'Mr Jones has eloped, I regret to say, to Tasmania; leaving 12 little Jones, and a possible 13th to Mrs Jones; most regrettable, most unfortunate, and yet not wholly an action to which one has no private key of one's own so to speak.'

* *The Flight of the Mind: The Letters of Virginia Woolf*, vol. 1: *1888–1912*, ed. Nigel Nicolson (London: Hogarth Press, 1975) p. 306.

NOTE

Virginia Woolf (1882–1941), novelist and essayist. The extract is taken from a letter to Violet Dickinson dated 25 August 1907.

   1. See p. 25.

James Addresses the Young*

HUGH WALPOLE

He was not aware that his long, slow, careful speech-windings were anything unusual or out of the way. I remember once, when staying with him at Rye, that, walking on a golf-course, we encountered two small children. James gave them some money with which to buy sweets but, when he had given it, began an oration to them as to what they should do with their money, the *kind* of sweets they should buy, the best time of day for the consumption of sweets and so on. They listened for a long time, staring up into his smooth Abbé-like face, then cast the coins on the ground and ran, screaming.

He was greatly distressed by this. What had frightened them? What had they seen or heard?

* 'Henry James: a Reminiscence', pp. 74–5.

NOTE

On Hugh Walpole, see p. 25. This anecdote is also recounted by Jessie Conrad, wife of the novelist Joseph Conrad:

Some three or four little girls caught his attention, and in his most ingratiating manner he stopped to talk to them. He began by presenting each with some pence and then proceeded to harangue them far above their understanding. The kiddies at last flung the coins on the ground and burst into loud sobbing before they ran away. (*Joseph Conrad and his Circle* (London: Jarrolds, 1935) p. 115)

Mrs Conrad locates the incident 'near his home in Rye'.

James on Tennyson, Shakespeare and George Sand*

JOHN BAILEY

[13 June 1908] Old Henry James, with his odd slowness, has given me some delightful talks; of which I only note his feelings of the mediocrity and narrowness of Tennyson – the one thing in which he vexed me – and I think he is all wrong, though, of course, there is a bourgeois limited side of Tennyson. H. James said the impression of America to him, in winter at any rate, was one of *ugliness, ugliness* – he repeated it in a kind of groan! – but on the other hand he said it was interesting to meet men who had never thought of themselves as belonging to any class – a thing impossible in feudal Europe. He talked to me in the church of Stratford of the inscrutable mystery of Shakespeare: the works on the one side and, on the other, that dull face, and all the stories we know of the man; 'commonplace; commonplace; almost degrading'.[1]

[11 October 1914] Old Henry James asked me to come and see him and was extraordinarily affectionate, kissing me on both cheeks when I arrived and thanking me enormously for coming. He is passionately English and says it is almost good that we were so little prepared, as it makes our moral position so splendid. He almost wept as he spoke. He says America is enthusiastically with us.... We talked then of many other things; of George Sand, of whom he said: 'She was a man ... a woman can transform herself into a man, but never into a gentleman!'

[13 February 1923] I had a good talk with Sargent[2] about Henry James, whom he knew very well. He told me, apropos of H. J.'s hatred of

* *John Bailey, 1864–1931: Letters & Diaries* (London: John Murray, 1935) pp. 111–12, 152–3, 222.

Americanisms, of a scene at which he had been present when a young American girl, being asked if she would have sugar with her tea, said, 'Oh yes, please pass me the sugar basin and I will fix it.' On which H. J. with horror, 'My dear young lady, will you kindly tell me what you will fix it with, and what you will fix it to!'

NOTES

1. James and Bailey were at this time fellow-guests at the home of Sir George and Lady Trevelyan at Welcombe, near Stratford-on-Avon. James had written on Shakespeare in his story 'The Birthplace', published in *The Better Sort* (1903). He also wrote an introduction to *The Tempest* for an edition of Shakespeare by Sir Sidney Lee published in 1907.

2. See p. 15.

'As If He Were Reading Proof'*

W. L. PHELPS

I first saw Henry James in 1911 in New Haven. He had been staying with some friends in Farmington, Conn., and he seemed to enjoy motor trips more than anything else. Miss Pope, who brought him from Farmington in her motor car, said that if she asked him if he would like to meet some people at a luncheon, he would say No; but if she suggested a journey in an automobile, he gladly agreed to that, and never asked whither they were going. Accordingly on this day, 23 May 1911, she brought him from Farmington to New Haven, where he was the guest of honour at a luncheon given by Mr and Mrs Harry Day. . . .

I had supposed that Mr James would be reserved and remote, difficult to talk with; on the contrary, he was absolutely charming. He made me feel immediately at ease, and as if we had been intimate friends. 'Come

* *Autobiography with Letters* (New York: Oxford University Press, 1939) pp. 550–2, 553, 554.

and sit here with me on the sofa', he said, and put his arm affectionately around my shoulder. I had with me a copy of his book *The Turn of the Screw* and I told him that although his literary style had often been called obscure, there was something else in his work that was even more difficult to read. 'And what is that?' 'That is your handwriting.' He smiled and took pains to write his name very slowly and distinctly in my copy of his book. I told him I thought *The Turn of the Screw* was the most terrifying ghost story I had ever read; that I read it when it first appeared, late at night, and when I had finished it, I did not dare go down stairs and put out the hall light. However, as I did not wish to leave the gas burning all night, there was a struggle between my Yankee parsimony and my fear of the dark. Finally I got my wife to stand at the head of the staircase. 'Don't you go away for a moment! don't you take your eyes off me; for if you do, I'll never get this light out!' I extinguished it and raced upstairs as if the devil and all his angels were after me.

Mr James expressed delight. 'Do you know, I wrote that story with the intention of terrifying every reader, and in the course of its composition, I thought it would be a total failure. I dictated every word of it to a Scot, who never from first to last betrayed the slightest emotion, nor did he ever make any comment. I might have been dictating statistics. I would dictate some phrase that I thought was blood-curdling; he would quietly take this down, look up at me and in a dry voice, say "What next?"'

It has been wittily said that Henry James conversed as if he were reading proof. This is really true. In desultory conversation on that day and on another occasion in England, he would stop in the middle of a sentence, feeling around in his mind for the right word; if he could not find it, he would abruptly change the subject, rather than use what he regarded as not quite the accurate or suitable word.

The next time I saw Henry James was on Saturday afternoon, 1 June 1912 in London, at a tea given by the English novelist, Mrs W. K. Clifford;[1] only Henry James and May Sinclair[2] were present. The conversation turned on the novels of Thomas Hardy; and I expressed my feelings of many years before, when I read *Tess* for the first time. The events and persons in that story seemed so real to me, and the catastrophe so overwhelming, that for days after I had finished it, I could not shake off my depression. Miss Sinclair said that the same sense of reality impressed her in reading the novels of Mrs Humphry Ward. This appalled Henry James, who said, '*May Sinclair, May Sinclair*, such a remark may do credit to your heart, but where does it leave your head?'

Drawn off into a corner of the room by Henry James, I spoke of testing a written style by reading it aloud; that I had found many passages in

Browning which seemed obscure to the eye were transparently clear when I read them aloud. To my surprise, he became excited. With intense earnestness he whispered in my ear, 'I have never in my life written a sentence that I did not mean to be read aloud, that I did not specifically intend to meet that test; you try it and see. Only don't you tell'. . . .

Lady Ritchie[3] (Thackeray's daughter) told me a good story about Henry James. One day as she was entering Paddington Station and was carrying under her arm a copy of a novel by him, she had the good fortune to meet him. 'Look, Henry James, here I am carrying one of your works to read on the train, and I meet the author himself!' He simulated dismay. 'My dear Lady Ritchie, what bad luck for you! Don't you know that you have there a copy of the most expensive edition of that work, and a new edition has just been issued for six shillings?' 'Don't you worry about that, Henry James. I just bought this at a second-hand bookstall for *one* shilling.' . . .

Mrs Edith Wharton told me that once at a dinner-party where Henry James was among the guests, a message came from a newspaper asking her if she would verify a rumour. She read the message aloud to the assembled party – 'Are you and Henry James engaged to be married?' The silence was broken by Henry James, exclaiming 'And yet they say truth is stranger than fiction!'

NOTES

William Lyon Phelps (1865–1943), American scholar and author, was Professor of English Literature at Yale University, 1901–33. He met Henry James on 23 May 1911 at a lunch party in New Haven, and saw him again in London in 1912. James described him as 'the boring and vacuous (though so well-meaning) Yale chatterbox Phelps'.

1. See p. 25.
2. May Sinclair (?1865–1946), English novelist.
3. Lady Anne Ritchie (1837–1919), eldest daughter of W. M. Thackeray, published novels and memoirs.

'In Great Form'*

MAX BEERBOHM

I met old Henry himself several times: he has become one of the stock ornaments of dinner-tables, uniform with Sargent,[1] Claude Phillips,[2] etc., – though he insists on being regarded as a recluse; and, wherever he is, nobody is *supposed* to see him there. All the same, he is in great form, really delightful to be with – though he hasn't a good word to say for anyone. I particularly want to read him on the subject of Arnold Bennett, of whose *Hilda Lessways*[3] he said (but will perhaps not put in writing) that it was 'like the slow squeezing-out of a big, dirty sponge'. He was splendid about a production of *Hamlet* by William Poel[4] at the Little Theatre. Somebody had taken him to see it, and I asked him what it was like. 'Like? Like? It was like Morning Prayers in a work-house!'

* David Cecil, *Max* (London: Constable, 1964) pp. 329–30.

NOTES

Sir Max Beerbohm (1872–1956), English critic, essayist and caricaturist. He knew James for about twenty years; for his first impressions of James, see Introduction. They met frequently on social occasions, but the friendship was never close. According to Leon Edel, James 'was of two minds about Max. He liked his praise and his wit; at the same time he experienced the element of hostility implicit in caricature and parody even when it also contains a large measure of affection' (*Master*, p. 395). Beerbohm wrote several parodies of James, reviewed two of his plays, and did nineteen major caricatures of him between 1898 and 1954 (listed in Rupert Hart-Davis, *A Catalogue of the Caricatures of Max Beerbohm* (London: Macmillan, 1972); see also *Beerbohm's Literary Caricatures*, ed. J. G. Riewald (Hamden, Conn.: Archon Books, 1977) pp. 224–35). On his parody of James in *A Christmas Garland*, and James's reaction to it, see p. 58; and for Beerbohm's comment on Sargent's portrait of James, see p. 145. The extract quoted is from a letter to Reginald Turner and records a meeting with James during a visit to London in 1914.

1. See p. 15.
2. See p. 30.
3. Novel by Arnold Bennett published in 1911.
4. William Poel (1852–1934), English theatrical producer.

James Reads Poetry*

EDITH WHARTON

I had never heard Henry James read aloud – or known that he enjoyed doing so – till one night some one alluded to Emily Brontë's poems, and I said I had never read 'Remembrance'. Immediately he took the volume from my hand, and, his eyes filling, and some far-away emotion deepening his rich and flexible voice, he began:

> Cold in the earth, and the deep snow piled above thee,
> Far, far removed, cold in the dreary grave,
> Have I forgot, my only Love, to love thee,
> Severed at last by Time's all-severing ways?

I had never before heard poetry read as he read it; and I never have since. He chanted it, and he was not afraid to chant it, as many good readers are, who, though they instinctively feel that the genius of the English poetical idiom requires it to be spoken *as poetry*, are yet afraid of yielding to their instinct because the present-day fashion is to chatter high verse as though it were colloquial prose. James, on the contrary, far from shirking the rhythmic emphasis, gave it full expression. His stammer ceased as by magic as soon as he began to read, and his ear, so sensitive to the convolutions of an intricate prose style, never allowed him to falter over the most complex prosody, but swept him forward on great rollers of sound till the full weight of his voice fell on the last cadence.

James's reading was a thing apart, an emanation of his inmost self, unaffected by fashion or elocutionary artifice. He read from his soul, and no one who never heard him read poetry knows what that soul was. Another day some one spoke of Whitman, and it was a joy to me to discover that James thought him, as I did, the greatest of American poets. *Leaves of Grass*[1] was put into his hands, and all that evening we sat

---

*A Backward Glance, pp. 185–6.

rapt while he wandered from 'The Song of Myself' to 'When Lilacs Last in the Door-yard Bloomed' (when he read 'Lovely and Soothing Death' his voice filled the hushed room like an organ adagio), and thence let himself be lured on to the mysterious music of 'Out of the Cradle', reading, or rather crooning it in a mood of subdued ecstasy till the five-fold invocation to Death tolled out like the knocks in the opening bars of the Fifth Symphony.

James's admiration of Whitman, his immediate response to that mighty appeal, was a new proof of the way in which, above a certain level, the most divergent intelligences walk together like gods. We talked long that night of *Leaves of Grass*, tossing back and forth to each other treasure after treasure; but finally James, in one of his sudden humorous drops from the heights, flung up his hands and cried out with the old stammer and twinkle: 'Oh, yes, a great genius; undoubtedly a very great genius! Only one cannot help deploring his too-extensive acquaintance with the foreign languages.'

NOTE

On Edith Wharton, see p. 27.
1. Whitman's volume of poems was published in 1855.

Part VI

The War and the End

'The *Angina Pectoris* . . . Unrelenting'*

EDMUND GOSSE

Henry James was here yesterday, and was much pleased to have news of you. He is looking much better, but the *angina pectoris* is there, unrelenting, and he goes nowhere without the strange exploding specific they now give at the moment of paroxysm. Sargent's portrait[1] of Henry James is nearly finished, and I hear is a masterpiece. There is a plaid waistcoat in it, heaving like a sea in storm, which is said to be prodigious.

* Evan Charteris, *The Life and Letters of Sir Edmund Gosse* (London: Heinemann, 1931) p. 349.

NOTE

On Edmund Gosse, see p. 10. The extract is from a letter to Thomas Hardy written from Gosse's home (17 Hanover Terrace) on 17 June 1913.

1. Sargent's fine portrait of James had been commissioned by a group of the latter's friends and admirers to honour his seventieth birthday and was painted in the spring of 1913 (the artist refused to accept any fee). James said that it depicted him 'all large and luscious rotundity – by which you may see how true a thing it is'. He bequeathed it to the National Portrait Gallery, where it now hangs. Max Beerbohm's verdict on the portrait was that it was 'a dead failure, a good presentment of a butler on holiday; but no more' (quoted by John Felstiner, *The Lies of Art* (New York: Knopf, 1973) p. 155).

James and England*

LOGAN PEARSALL SMITH

'Our dear Howard', Henry James wrote of his loved Howard Sturgis, 'is like a richly sugared cake always on the table. We sit round him in a

* 'Slices of Cake', *New Statesman*, XXV (5 June 1943) pp. 367–8.

circle and help ourselves. Now and then we fling a slice over our shoulders to somebody outside.'

Henry James was a cake, of course, even more richly spiced and sugared; and as I am almost the last of the guests who sat on golden chairs round that table, I have been asked to dole out a few slices. The first slice I can now fling comes from the table of Mrs Humphry Ward, whose house in Grosvenor Place Edith Wharton rented, shortly after the outbreak of the war in 1914. I was asked to meet Henry James at luncheon there, and into the room he burst, his great eyes ablaze.

'My hands, I must wash them!' he cried, 'my hands are dripping with blood. All the way from Chelsea to Grosvenor Place I have been bayoneting, my dear Edith, and hurling bombs and ravishing and raping. It is my daydream to squat down with King George of England, with the President of the French Republic and the Czar of Russia on the Emperor William's belly, until we squeeze out of it the last irrevocable drops of bitter retribution.'

Mrs Wharton, who had come over in a blaze from Paris, said that she must have a seat with the others. 'No, Edith,' was the stern reply of this august septuagenarian, 'that imperial stomach is no seat for ladies. This is a war for men only: it is a war for me and poor Logan.'

'But surely we must discriminate,' I mildly suggested to this master of discriminations, 'surely we must look to the right and left, and proceed, all eyes, with care and strategical caution. This is certainly my war, as I am a naturalised British subject; but you, I believe, are a neutral, as neutral as Switzerland or Sweden. Why don't you come into it?' I asked him, as, panting, he paused to wipe the imagined gore from his face,' why don't you enrol yourself as a British subject?'

More than once, during the winter that followed, I would end with this trumpet-note my colloquies with Henry James on the telephone. 'When are you coming into the war?' I would hiss; 'how long are you going to sit with the Roumanians on a back seat in the Balkans?'

One day the elaborations of phrase, the parentheses, the polysyllabic evasions, which made a talk on the telephone with Henry James so amazing an adventure, were replaced by a terse query.

'Logan, how – you know what I mean – how do you do it?'

'You go,' I tersely replied, 'to a solicitor.'

'Of course. I know just the right person': and this great man of action rang off with a bang that must almost have smashed the receiver. . . .

Most disconcerting, had I found a remark of George Santayana's,[1] to the effect that he would never cross the Channel again, owing to the rapid Americanisation of England. With these words ringing in my ears (for I had just heard them) I broke the silence between myself and my Chelsea neighbour on one of our walks in this riverside suburb. 'Of course,' I said, 'you know Santayana?'

'Oh, of course,' replied Henry James, 'wasn't Santayana a great friend of my brother William at Harvard? I know his friends; I know his crystal-clear prose; and what you never find in other writers to-day, the touch here and there of the fiddle or the note of the nightingale. I know his thought, as far as a humble old dreamer like myself can know it. I know at any rate the lofty realms where he walks among the high places of European philosophy.'

'Then you must often have met him?'

'My dear fellow, I tell you I have spent days, have spent months in his company. I have listened, and listened long, to the sound of his enchanting conversation.'

'The most enchanting in the world, of course', I answered. 'So you know him personally; he comes to see you when he is in London?'

'To answer your question, my dear Logan, as plainly – and I may say, as brutally – as you put it, I have *not* personally (to use your blunt adverb) met Santayana; nor shall I ever meet him. He has never rung my doorbell, nor will he ever ring it. He wouldn't ring it even if he were in London; and now he isn't seen in London any more.'

'But I saw him yesterday; he is now here in person, and is lunching with me tomorrow. Though you don't like blunt questions, I shall permit myself bluntly to ask you, will you come to luncheon to meet him?'

'Come!' Henry James cried, raising his hands to Heaven. 'I would walk across London with bare feet on the snow to meet George Santayana.[2] At what time? One-thirty! I will come. At one-thirty I shall inevitably, inexorably make my appearance!'

He was only a minute or two late; as my sisters and I were shaking hands with Santayana, we saw a taxi drive up. Then we heard heavy footsteps on the stairs, and there was a pause before the drawing-room door opened, and the most portentous of all the personalities I have ever encountered momentously entered. With a rudeness which was perfectly right (for on grave occasions the small coin of good manners must be treated as trash) he ignored us all but the Spanish hildago, whom he gravely approached, and laying his arm on his shoulder, 'Now tell me,' he almost reproachfully queried, 'are you really George Santayana?' When fully reassured on this point, he turned to the rest of us with greetings of elaborate but quite unapologetic courtesy; and we all went into luncheon.

Our talk was about England. I expressed my life-long satisfaction in

being domiciled with so superior a race as the English. 'Yes,' the
Spaniard agreed, 'in my opinion the most superior white race, since the
Greeks, which has peopled this planet.'

And yet, and yet, wasn't Santayana about to say farewell to this island
for ever? And hadn't our other guest just received two bluff, British
slaps? He had certainly been trounced, but a few months ago, by a moral
thinker and bestselling novelist, who, in a book called *Boon*, had pilloried
his old friend and held him up to public derision. And the year before,
enraged British females, with a ferocity even greater than the author of
Boon – the 'phrophet', as Henry James called Wells – had slashed with a
knife the great face of his exhibited portrait, and had tried to cut it to
pieces. Wasn't it possible that these two encounters with British Philis-
tinism, joined with the unmentionably awful ordeal and yelled-at exposure when he stood before the theatrical curtain in the Nineties; wasn't it
possible, or even probable, that such misadventures might have caused
the correct author of so many exquisitely well-bred stories to cast a
backward, and perhaps a rueful glance, at the amenity of his previous
un-English freedom? Could a prudish and well-conducted old gentleman swallow without gulping what Henry James had been forced to
swallow?

Having a personal interest in the question, and remembering my own
former qualms, I adumbrated a query. Was there any loyalty or transfer
of allegiance which could be whole-heartedly accepted without reserva-
tion? Mustn't such things, like all that is mortal, be subject to qualifications, to occasional drawbacks, and even to moments, at least, of
disillusion?

In silence our august guest pondered my question; nor did Henry
James ever impress one as more awe-inspiringly august than in his
moments of wordless rumination. He now seemed to be silently shaking
(to borrow one of his own metaphors) the bottle into which life had
poured for him the wine of experience; shaking it to taste what lees might
be stirred by this oscillation. 'Disillusion?' no, that was not the word to
be used of his experiences with regard to those decent and dauntless
people. Though much too magnanimous to speak of, or even perhaps to
remember, the slaps in the face I have mentioned, he still hesitated over
the word 'drawback'. Well, perhaps there were drawbacks, and especially the one which had forced Edith Wharton to depart from the shores of
this island. The numbness and dumbness of tongue-tied people of
England! No good talk, no good general conversation, none of that
famous co-operative criticism of life, which was the solace of existence in
France and in Italy. 'No house any longer in London where fine spirits

could gather and wag their tongues freely. No echo of Holland House, nor even of the shoddy Blessington salon. No tirades, no denunciations; nothing but dreary mumblings and grumblings about politics, diseases and dentists, and insipid duologues automatically turned on and switched off at vapid luncheons and dinners.'

As we four sat round that great cake or, as it were, Christmas confection; as the candles upon it seemed to burn more and more brightly till there was a final outpouring of ignited spirit, I felt that this great combustion was no impromptu performance, but something that was being developed to lead up, for this company and this occasion, to a climax. An anti-climax it seemed. And yet wasn't it in a way a climax? Henry James's voice dropped to a conversational level.

'I am now going to tell you a story,' he said, 'it's a story I have never told before, and shall never tell again; a story that in decency I never ought to tell.

'But now I shall indecently tell it!

'Some years ago my friend Alphonse Daudet[3] was in London; he often came to see me, and we met at dinners and luncheons. On the last of these occasions when he came to say farewell, "My dear friend" he remarked, "I have been observing you carefully for some months; I have met almost all your friends and acquaintances; *et je vois que vous demeurez parmi des gens moins fins que vous.*" That was what he said when he left England for Paris. Oh, for the wings of the dove, I sigh sometimes to follow after him, and after Edith, to that conversational city! But I see I have lingered too late in this pleasant society; at my age one is apt to prolong one's happiest moments. I hadn't the slightest notion how the clock had been ticking. Do you think, Logan, that you could ring up for a taxi for me?'

NOTES

Logan Pearsall Smith (1865–1946), American author, spent most of his life in England. His books include *Words and Idioms* (1925) and three collections of *Trivia* (1918–33). He spent a weekend at Lamb House in the summer of 1913; after he left, James wrote that 'Logan Pearsall Smith was just with me for 36 hours – and the tide of gossip between us rose high, he being a great master of that effect.'

1. George Santayana (1863–1952) was Professor of Philosophy at Harvard from 1889 until 1912; from 1914 he lived in Europe.

2. Leon Edel, who regards Smith as an unreliable witness, has commented on this account as follows: 'Actually what James had written to Gaillard Lapsley

was "I envy you the intercourse of Santayana, whom I don't know and have never seen, but whose admirable mind and style I so prize that I wish greatly he sometimes came to London"' (*Master*, p. 497).

3. Alphonse Daudet (1840–97), French novelist. James formed a friendship with him during his residence in Paris and entertained him when Daudet visited London in 1895. He included an essay on Daudet in his *Partial Portraits* (1888) and in 1890 published a translation of Daudet's *Port Tarascon.*

'Uncontrollable Anger'*

MRS BELLOC LOWNDES

The outbreak of the first European war gave Henry James a shock from which he never even partially recovered.... I believe the War was present to his mind during every waking moment of the day....

I only once saw Henry James really angry. In the early summer of 1914, Hugh Walpole,[1] who had been having trouble with his eyes, told me he was going to Russia.... When war started early that August, he had made all his plans to leave England, and he did not allow what had just happened to affect those plans. The following winter, Henry James and I happened to meet in the house of a well-known London hostess, who spoke with scorn of the fact that immediately on the outbreak of war Walpole had left his country. I at once said it was within my knowledge that he had made all his plans for going to Russia before there had been any thought of war, and that the state of his eyesight would have made it impossible for him to join the Army. She refused to take either, or both, of these reasons as an excuse. Henry James was so angry that, suddenly seizing my arm, he muttered, 'Let you and me who are friends of Walpole leave this house!' And when we were in the street I saw he was still shaken with what seemed uncontrollable anger....

On another occasion I suddenly felt impelled to tell him how much genuine happiness my friendship with him had brought into my life. I said, 'Of course I know why you are so kind to me.' He answered at once, in French, 'Surely the reason is that you are you, and I am I?' I

* *The Merry Wives of Westminster* (London: Macmillan, 1946) pp. 193–4, 139–40, 186–7.

exclaimed, 'There is a much better reason than that! The real reason is surely because I am the only writer of your acquaintance who has never sent you one of his or her books. How you must groan as the parcels come in.'

He observed, in a somewhat shamefaced voice, 'You are the only human being who has ever guessed – shall I say, ah me, what the coming of those parcels – those kind, those generous, those gracious gifts – means to their grateful, their often embarrassed, their sometimes perplexed, recipient!' – and then his voice died away.

NOTE

Mrs Belloc Lowndes was the pseudonym of Mrs Marie Adelaide Lowndes (1868–1947), novelist. She was the wife of Frederic S. Lowndes and a sister of Hilaire Belloc.

1. See p. 25.

'Transfigured'*

EDMUND GOSSE

The record of the last months of Henry James's life is told in the wonderful letters that he wrote between the beginning of August 1914, and the close of November 1915. He was at Rye when the war broke out, but he found it absolutely impossible to stay there without daily communication with friends in person, and, contrary to his lifelong habit, he came posting up to London in the midst of the burning August weather. He was transfigured by the events of those early weeks, overpowered, and yet, in his vast and generous excitement, himself overpowering. He threw off all the languor and melancholy of the recent years, and he appeared actually grown in size as he stalked the streets, amazingly moved by the unexpected nightmare, 'the huge horror of blackness' which he saw before him. 'The plunge of civilisation into the abyss of blood and darkness by the wanton feat of these two infamous autocrats'

* 'Henry James', *London Mercury*, II (1920) pp. 38–9.

made him suddenly realise that the quiet years of prosperity which had preceded 1914 had been really, as he put it, 'treacherous', and that their perfidy had left us unprotected against the tragic terrors which now faced our world. It was astonishing how great Henry James suddenly seemed to become; he positively loomed above us in his splendid and disinterested faith. His first instinct had been horror at the prospect; his second anger and indignation against the criminals; but to these succeeded a passion of love and sympathy for England and France, and an unyielding but anxious and straining confidence in their ultimate success. Nothing could express this better than the language of a friend who saw him constantly and studied his moods with penetrating sympathy. Mr Percy Lubbock[1] says:

> To all who listened to him in those days it must have seemed that he gave us what we lacked – a voice; there was a trumpet note in it that was heard nowhere else and that alone rose to the height of the truth.

The impression Henry James gave in these first months of the war could not be reproduced in better terms. To be in his company was to be encouraged, stimulated and yet filled with a sense of the almost intolerable gravity of the situation; it was to be moved with that 'trumpet note' in his voice, as the men fighting in the dark defiles of Roncevaux were moved by the sound of the oliphant of Roland. He drew a long breath of relief in the thought that England had not failed in her manifest duty to France, or 'shirked any one of the implications of the Entente'. When, as at the end of the first month, things were far from exhilarating for the Allies, Henry James did not give way to despair, but he went back to Rye, possessing his soul in waiting patience, 'bracing himself unutterably', as he put it, 'and holding on somehow (though to God knows what!) in presence of the perpetrations so gratuitously and infamously hideous as the destruction of Louvain and its accompaniments.'

At Lamb House he sat through that gorgeous tawny September, listening to the German guns thundering just across the Channel, while the advance of the enemy through those beautiful lands which he knew and loved so well filled him with anguish. He used to sally forth and stand on the bastions of his little town, gazing over the dim marsh that became sand-dunes, and then sea, and then a mirage of the white cliffs of French Flanders that were actually visible when the atmosphere grew transparent. The anguish of his execration became almost the howl of some animal, of a lion of the forest with the arrow in his flank, when the Germans wrecked Reims Cathedral. He gazed and gazed over the sea south-east, and almost fancied that he saw the flicker of the flames. He ate and drank, he talked and walked and thought, he slept and waked and lived and breathed only the War. His friends grew anxious, the tension was beyond what his natural powers, transfigured as they were, could be expected to endure, and he was persuaded to come back to Chelsea, although a semblance of summer still made Rye attractive.

NOTE

On Gosse, see p. 10.
  1. See p. 50.

'A *Beau Geste*'*

MRS HUMPHRY WARD

I will record here the last time but one that I ever saw Henry James – a vision, an impression, which the retina of memory will surely keep to the end. It was at Grosvenor Place in the autumn of 1915, the second year of the war. How doubly close by then he had grown to all our hearts! His passionate sympathy for England and France, his English naturalisation – a *beau geste* indeed, but so sincere, so moving – the pity and wrath that carried him to sit by wounded soldiers, and made him put all literary work aside as something not worth doing, so that he might spend time and thought on helping the American ambulance in France – one must supply all this as the background of the scene.

It was a Sunday afternoon. Our London house had been let for a time, but we were in it again for a few weeks, drawn into the rushing tide of war-talk and war anxieties. The room was full when Henry James came in. I saw that he was in a stirred, excited mood, and the key to it was soon found. He began to repeat the conversation of an American envoy to Berlin – a well-known man – to whom he had just been listening. He described first the envoy's impression of the German leaders, political

* *A Writer's Recollections*, pp. 330–1.

and military, of Berlin. 'They seemed to him like men waiting in a room from which the air is being slowly exhausted. They *know* they can't win! It is only a question of how long, and how much damage they can do.' The American further reported that after his formal business had been done with the Prussian Foreign Minister, the Prussian – relaxing his whole attitude and offering a cigarette – said – 'Now then let me talk to you frankly, as man to man!' – and began a bitter attack on the attitude of President Wilson. Colonel —— listened, and when the outburst was done, said – 'Very well! Then I too will speak frankly. I have known President Wilson for many years. He is a very strong man, physically and morally. You can neither frighten him, nor bluff him –'

And then – springing up in his seat – 'And, by Heaven, if you want war with America, you can have it to-morrow!'

Mr James's dramatic repetition of this story, his eyes on fire, his hand striking the arm of his chair, remains with me as my last sight of him in a typical representative moment.

NOTE

On Mrs Humphry Ward, see p. 42.

The Order of Merit*

JAMES S. BAIN

Sir Edmund Gosse, one of his closest friends, himself told me this ... story.... He had asked leave to tell Henry James of the award [of the Order of Merit], but, on entering the sick-room, he found his friend lying with closed eyes, in the flickering light of a single candle, and the nurse told him she was afraid the patient was past hearing anything. Leaning on the bed, Gosse whispered, 'Henry, they've given you the OM', but not a sign of interest showed in the still face, and Gosse quietly left the room. Directly the door closed Henry James opened his eyes and said, 'Nurse, take away the candle and spare my blushes.'

* *A Bookseller Looks Back* (London: Macmillan, 1940) pp. 221–2.

NOTE

After his naturalisation as a British subject, James became eligible for the Order of Merit – an honour in the gift of the Crown and the highest that can be bestowed on an author. On 18 December 1915 Edward Marsh, who was attached to the Prime Minister's office, wrote a memorandum to Asquith urging that the OM should be given to James. Asquith acted quickly, the royal assent followed, and the news was made public on 1 January 1916. Max Beerbohm's 'The Guerdon', a superb parody of James's later style, describes an imagined interview between the King and the Lord Chamberlain, both of whom are very vague as to who Henry James might be (reprinted in *Parodies*, ed. Dwight Macdonald (London: Faber, 1961) pp. 147–9).

James's Funeral*

EDMUND GOSSE

The group of friends, a large company, who gathered in Old Chelsea Church this afternoon, must have included several whose thoughts went back, like mine, to the mysterious and poignant story which Henry James contrived to publish twenty-five years ago.... As we stood round the shell of that incomparable brain, of that noble and tender heart, it flashed across me that to generations yet unawakened to a knowledge of his value Old Chelsea Church must for ever be the Altar of the Dead.

No man has awakened greater loyalty or penetrated so many shy spirits with affection. But ... when the war with Germany broke out he ceased to be merely the idol of an esoteric group. He became a soldier; he belonged to England. No one has suffered more in spirit, no one was more tensely agitated by the war, than Henry James.... Quite in the beginning of August 1914, he said to two English friends, 'However British you may be, I am more British still.'

* *The Times*, 4 March 1916, p. 7.

NOTE

The extract is taken from a letter dated 3 March 1916 and addressed to the Editor of *The Times*. The issue of the newspaper in which it appeared also carried the headlines 'Lost British Ships' and 'New Call to Married Men Expected'.

Index